THE GOLDEN BLADE

TOGETHER ON EARTH

1999

51st EDITION

Anthroposophy springs from the work and teaching of Rudolf Steiner. He described it as a path of knowledge, to guide the spiritual in the human being to the spiritual in the universe.

The aim of this annual journal is to bring the outlook of anthroposophy to bear on questions and activities relevant to the present, in a way which may have lasting value. It was founded in 1949 by Charles Davy and Arnold Freeman, who were its first editors.

The title derives from an old Persian legend, according to which King Jamshid received from his god, Ahura Mazda, a golden blade with which to fulfil his mission on earth. It carried the heavenly forces of light into the darkness of earthly substance, thus allowing its transformation. The legend points to the possibility that humanity, through wise and compassionate work with the earth, can one day regain on a new level what was lost when the Age of Gold was supplanted by those of Silver, Bronze and Iron. Technology could serve this aim; instead of endangering our planet's life, it could help to make the earth a new sun.

TOGETHER ON EARTH

Edited by William Forward, Simon Blaxland-de Lange
and Andrew Wolpert

The Golden Blade

First published in 1998 by The Golden Blade

The Golden Blade
Emerson College
Forest Row
East Sussex RH18 5JX
England

ISBN 0-9531600-1-7
ISSN 0967-6708

Printed in Great Britain
by Design To Print, Forest Row, East Sussex

Contents

Editorial Notes

As the inner harvest of 1998 is being gathered in, it is already apparent that this year has lived up to the expectation – referred to in our previous Editorial Notes – that it could create favourable conditions for the machinations of that dragon whose plans are brought closer to fulfilment through the sowing of fear in the hearts and minds of human beings. 1998 will quite likely go down in history as a year in which the long-imminent destabilisation of the Western world's socio-political arena became a reality. Especially with the economic and political melt-down in Russia, it is clear that the old-established social forms based on a human soul-configuration antecedent to the incarnation of the spirit-bearing ego – the consciousness or spiritual soul – have altogether lost all outward respect and sovereignty. This is because these essentially dualistic social forms – with their familiar antitheses such as Right and Left wing – do not reckon with the vital thrust of that third force of individual responsibility which is cherished by growing numbers of people today.

As editors of this journal we take it for granted that our readers are seeking to promote this third force rather than hoping a great leader will come along and bring outward order to the chaos. Rather than dwell therefore on phenomena that are a reflection of this disintegration, we have chosen to carry the theme of destiny, karma and reincarnation that has underlain the two previous issues into the wider context of outer life. What social forms further or hinder the possibility of our exploring these destiny-questions together? What kind of relationship to the Earth (and hence to the land itself) is called for if we seek to do this work? What contribution can the Anthroposophical Society make to the fashioning of both these social forms and this relationship? These are the kinds of questions we have invited our contributors to address in the hope that a collection of such articles might – from their very diverse standpoints – contribute towards the forming of a source of encouragement and light to those who have found themselves navigating increasingly stormy seas in the course of 1998.

John Alexandra launches straight into the central focus of our theme with the opening words of his article, in which he analyses some of the main dilemmas of modern life from this standpoint, while indicating that these problems are themselves the mainspring of the challenge to find solutions.

In his article on biodynamic farming, Manfred Klett takes a controversial view of the role of the farm within the economy. At the time of Rudolf Steiner's most intense work on the social question (1917 – 1919) he tended to refer to agriculture as working on fundamentally different principles from those of industry. Industry rightly aims to maximise output of products for minimum input of labour. This has an inherent tendency towards automation and mass-production, with the social consequence of emancipation and alienation from Nature. Agriculture, if rightly understood and pursued, involves integrating an ever larger part of the surrounding community into the processes of Nature: agriculture works within a given natural order. Steiner's efforts to bring about a re-organisation of society such as to recognise and accommodate the threefold nature of the human being were directed strongly towards the emancipated masses working in an industrialised, urban environment. The very environment where the absence of any humanly coherent order was most devastatingly evident. Here Klett is suggesting that the opening for social renewal can no longer be found in industrialised society, but must rather be sought in and around the small communities dedicated to the ideals of biodynamic farming. Bringing a spiritual impulse into agriculture has a transforming effect on the social environment of the farms involved.

Simon Blaxland – de Lange offers an analysis of modern life in terms of destiny groups or karmic streams, and emphasises the importance of a collaboration between them if new shoots are to emerge from the old exhausted forms. William Forward reminds us that our karmic communities include, and are indeed vitally dependant on, those who have died. Andrew Wolpert's article builds a bridge between individuals working with the Earth and earthly substance, and the general human task we have on Earth that is represented by the Anthroposophical Society. Ken Gibson examines how a karmic community of individuals come together at a time and in a place that enables them to engage in their task.

Fumiko Chikami's biographical article extends the compass of this collection to include Japan and the Far East, thus straddling the entire gamut of changes that have occurred between the community wisdom of the ancient East and its new potential in the individualised consciousness of modern times. Sibylle Eichstaedt concludes the sequence of articles with her description of one individual's search for her karmic community and the obstacles which, because of their very friendliness, can lie in the way.

Terry Boardman's review of Paul Emberson's book *From Gondhishapur to Silicon Valley* takes in a whole further dimension of the theme, namely, the crucial role that technology can play for good or ill in a society seeking its way into the future. The review of David Brown's book *Leonardo da Vinci* highlights the significance of a formative karmic connection in the origin of genius and acknowledges orthodox academic scholarship at its best.

There are certain matters of "House Style" that we have taken into consideration. Wherever possible and appropriate, we would like the deliberate personal conventions of our authors to remain unedited. Terry Boardman has used the word "anthroposopher", consciously wanting to avoid the connotations of "...ist". We respect that wish without necessarily sharing the reason behind it. We also wish to retain the option of avoiding politically correct usage if it burdens a text with excessive instances of "he/she", "his/her" alternatives. The whole question of the gender-free connotation of the word "man", and the all-human inclusive impulse of anthroposophy that should preclude suspicion of exclusions are matters that will become ever more urgent as the tyranny of a blanket ideology actually undermines the truths it purports to stand for.

We would like to express our gratitude to the Council of the Anthroposophical Society in Great Britain which has now decided to fund this journal's production costs. We very much appreciate the fact that *The Golden Blade* can continue with the support of the Society, and are very grateful for the opportunity to go on with this work.

S. B. d L.
W. F.
A. W.

Being born into a Brave New World

John Alexandra

Can I Still Be Born?

You arrive at the airport departure gate, to be greeted with the news: *No transatlantic flights for the foreseeable future.* This is the route you've always taken – many times before. And it's usually gone fine – in both directions. *Why not?* you ask. *No suitable housing is currently available there*, comes the stunning answer. *Their ecological damage is too serious.*

You are taken aback, to say the least. How can this have happened – and without warning?

Human souls arrive at the "departure gate," to be greeted with the news: *No "travel to Earth" for the foreseeable future.* This is the "route" they've always taken – many times before. And it's usually gone fine – in both directions. *Why not?* they ask. *No suitable bodies are currently available*, comes the stunning answer. *Their ecology is too seriously damaged.*

You're taken aback! How can this be – without warning?

Maybe we've had plenty of warning – but we've slept through it. How about Aldous Huxley's Brave New World? Remember the Alphas, the Betas, the Epsilons? The lab-rooms full of identical, cloned babies, all designed to fit their status in life? The Epsilons, with minimal intelligence so they will be happy sewage-workers? The Alpha Plus intellectuals who control the machinery of society – but are themselves also controlled by it? Brave New World is a Utopia populated by blissfully happy people who have everything they want. The only problem is, they are dehumanized – they can no longer unfold their unique, individual destiny. From "conception" on, they live fully programmed lives in a technologically controlled and manipulated society. While laboratory-executed reproduction is carefully designed to fit society's economic requirements, people's need for human interaction is provided by the "feelies," carefully controlled – and controlling – entertainment that provides tactile and other stimulation in addition to the visual and aural stimulation of today's movies.

What was Huxley's purpose? To show where the then existing scientific and societal tendencies *had* to take us. To a technological totalitarianism, where the "soil" in which people's humanity can grow has been destroyed, and where people are imprisoned in a dehumanized, technological societal structure. As Huxley himself observed, this Brave New World totalitarianism has a particular character: it comes unseen. People *welcome* the control because it is "inflicted" through the medium of comfort, pleasure and entertainment. This contrasts to George Orwell's 1984 (communist style) society, where people are controlled against their will by outer force, through fear and by inflicting pain and punishment.[1]

When Huxley wrote the book in 1931, he considered his dehumanized society to be a very distant fable – five or six hundred years away. A scant twenty-seven years later, he wrote Brave *New World Revisited* – and *radically* revised his estimate:

> *The nightmare of total organization which I had situated [five centuries ahead] has emerged from the safe, remote future and is now awaiting us, just around the next corner.*[2]

And that statement is forty years old – it's Paleolithic!

Both the technological and consciousness control aspects of Huxley's fable are no longer "just around the next corner," or even on our doorstep. They've moved in, and are rapidly taking over the house.

Systematic Damage To the Human Ecology

The dehumanizing forces Huxley recognized, which are still steadily and inexorably creating a Brave New World today, have a twofold effect:

- They transform (and recreate) the world outside us as fully programmed edifice – I call it the Technostructure that imprisons us as human beings. This totally organized structure is steadily replacing the world in which the individuality can meet the wise consequences of its previous actions. Within this edifice, B.F. Skinner inspired programmed procedures may reward or punish specific behaviours. But the guiding wisdom of destiny is totally excluded – it cannot permeate or transform the structure.
- They systematically destroy our "human ecology," by polluting and destroying the "soil" in which our humanity grows, the "water" which nourishes it, and the "air" it breathes. This, too, prevents us from unfolding our individual destiny, but through processes *within* the individual human being. The end result is a body which looks physically human and is able to function economically. In reality, however, it is a dehumanized shell that has lost the possibility, created over aeons, to provide a "home" where the individuality can unfold its unique destiny from life to life, in a body formed for this purpose.

These two aspects of the Brave New World assault go

hand in hand: every step in the destruction of the human ecology allows a further step in the building of the Technostructure – and vice versa. And although they function immensely cohesively, these dehumanizing forces come from a multitude of directions: economic, educational, medical, scientific, electronic and legal, as well as through the media and entertainment (to mention but a few). Even the greatest initiates may be unable to unfold fruitful incarnations in such ecologically damaged conditions.

Evidence of the increasing destruction of this human ecology abounds on every hand. Some years ago in the U.K., a two-year-old's skull was smashed with bricks and a metal bar; his body was then laid across a railroad track, where it was cut in half by a train. More recently, four girls and a beloved teacher were killed in an American schoolyard; it was a premeditated murder – the fire alarms had been deliberately activated so the children would have to enter the murderers' line of fire. Both crimes would have been horrific even if they had been committed by hardened criminals. But the alleged perpetrators of both atrocities were *young children:* in the British crime, two 10-year-olds; in the American, an 11-and a 13-year old. Such crimes by children would have been totally unthinkable even a few decades ago. Yet today they are not even isolated incidents. On the American continent alone, merely naming Springfield, OR, Edinboro, PA, Paducah, KY, or Pearl, MI stirs the memories of similar tragic mass murders committed by children just in recent months.[3]

What does it say about the damage to our human ecology that our *children* can commit such previously unthinkable crimes – routinely and around the world? Is the emergence of this new level of inhuman violence in our children not an inescapable "soil test," indicating how far this destruction of our individual humanity – and, therefore, the dehumanization of the whole of society – has already progressed?

Several authors have described different aspects of this dehumanization. Jane Healy's *Endangered Minds: Why Children Don't Think and What We Can Do About It* documents meticulously the increasing damage to children's growing brains and its effect on their ability to learn.[4] Dave Grossman's *On Killing: The Psychological Cost of Learning to Kill in War and Society* analyzes the process by which violence and killing have become so routine in our society.[5] My book, *Mephistopheles' Anvil: Forging a More Human Future*, examines our human ecological damage and the imprisonment of our consciousness within the Technostructure.[6] It shows how this dehumanization can only be counteracted through a major change in individual human consciousness, a change of the same order of magnitude as that of the Renaissance. Central to this transformation is the ability to confront the evils of society as a necessary challenge, an "anvil" against which we can forge the new spiritual faculties we need for our human evolutionary future.

Teaching Children To Enjoy Killing

What drives us to the characteristic Brave New World situation (embracing things that, initially, we strongly rejected as totally inhuman)? The process has three stages: First, the unthinkable becomes thinkable. Then it becomes acceptable. Finally, we welcome it. Let's examine this process in some characteristic situations: in violence and killing, in cloning, and in human interaction.

Turn to Grossman's book. Formerly a Lieutenant Colonel in the U.S. Army and an instructor at West Point Military Academy, he is currently Professor of Military Science at Arkansas State University (located, ironically, in Jonesboro, where the schoolyard murders took place). Do soldiers really *want* to kill? he asks. In World War II, the level of killing by infantry soldiers was a surprisingly low 15% to 20% (i.e., during any encounter between opposing troops, only 15 to 20 of every 100 soldiers were willing to fire their guns to kill another human being) – the underlying factor being the soldiers' inborn reluctance to kill. But an army cannot function with such a low a level of job efficiency, Grossman points out; something had to be done about it. By the Korean War, the army had taken major strides – the rate had tripled (to 55%). And by Vietnam, the killing score was almost perfect – 95%.

A dramatic increase in a mere thirty-year period. How had the army so effectively managed to suppress or destroy the cadets' humanity, so they would now be willing, or at least able, to kill so routinely? Grossman describes some of the "Clockwork Orange" training methods used to systematically desensitize the cadets, to immunize them against feeling the effects of killing. They were, for example, repeatedly forced to view movies specially designed to depict increasingly graphic violence and killings. By being desensitized through these films, the men's emotions eventually became dissociated from their own experiences. As these movies became progressively more horrific, the cadets' heads were bolted in clamps so they could not turn away; and their eyelids were prevented from closing by a special device.

The military no longer tolerates such methods. Yet remarkably, says Grossman, we civilians not only allow, but willingly use these same, horrendous methods on our own children, by regularly subjecting them to the desensitization and dehumanization of ever more violent movies and video games. We call it entertainment. Then we're surprised at the schoolyard murders.

Parenthetically, again we see the two aspects going hand

in hand: the destruction of the human ecology and the creation of outer tools of dehumanization, each "feeding" the other.

Human Cloning - It's with Us

As a second example, let's take the temperature on another aspect of *Brave New World* – cloned babies – an unthinkable piece of science fiction in 1931 (when Huxley wrote the book). By 1996, Dolly (the now-famous sheep) had been cloned. Her DNA and, therefore, all her essential character traits, are identical to those of her "predecessor." Using such techniques, we will eventually be able to create two identical twins, three identical triplets, or three thousand identical "tri-millets." During 1998, scientists in Hawaii used similar techniques to clone fifty mice.[7]

Dolly's cloning provoked an immediate hue and cry, with calls for legislation banning human cloning research. In the U.S., Bill Clinton responded "appropriately:" with immediate political action. He gave a federal bioethics panel ninety days to present proposals on whether and how human cloning should be banned or regulated.[8] The fifty Hawaiian mice – only two years later – brought no such hue and cry. The medical possibilities were emphasized (there was talk, for example, of organs being grown in pigs for human transplantation, eliminating dependence on human donors). By then, Dolly was a long-forgotten hot topic. The public had new hot buttons to push. This is stage two – letting the process go on.

In the not-too-distant future, we can be sure, these things will move to stage three: they'll be welcomed. The practical economic and self-interested choices will be compelling: *Do you really want a baby that may have a low IQ, be retarded, susceptible to breast cancer or Alzheimer's? Wouldn't you prefer one with a high IQ? Or one that will be great in basketball? The price tag is affordable – unless, of course, you want to buy Einstein's DNA; or Michael Jordan's. And you'll be making a significant contribution to the national economy.* How do you think people will respond? Who in their right mind will want an old-fashioned, take-what-you're-given baby?

Virtual Reality Feelies

What about the feelies – programmed human interaction? From Huxley's science fiction fantasy, these, too, have crossed today's horizon. Turn to Howard Rheingold's *Virtual Reality*.[9] This book documents many uses of the virtual reality technology, most of which are already available (or close to it). In most virtual reality applications, the user wears a headset that provides 3-D video images, together with a bodysuit that both provides tactile sensations and measures the wearer's slightest movements.

What are some of its uses? A doctor with a rare specialty today is limited to performing operations in places where she can be physically present. Using this technology, by contrast, she could perform operations on patients everywhere in the world – without leaving home. The patient would be operated on by a robot. The doctor, wearing the virtual reality suit, would operate on the computer image of the patient from "home." The suit would pick up the doctor's slightest movements in moving the surgical instruments. The robot would then mimic these movements to operate on the real patient.

Although still in its infancy, says Rheingold, a similar technology could be used for teledildonics – sex at a distance. Two individuals, each wearing a virtual reality suit, and again perhaps in different parts of the globe, could use this technology for "virtual sex." Each body suit would pick up the partner's slightest body movements and transmit them as tactile sensations to the other suit. One of the participants could also be a virtual person – a computer programmed to create the unique "partner of the person's dreams." This technology would be the modern equivalent – but in a completely individualized form – of Huxley's feelies.

Why might this technology be welcomed? In an era fixated on sexual harassment, "virtual sex" could go a long way towards eliminating the need for relationships between real women and men. The virtual partner would be free of all the complicating factors that a human partner inevitably brings. Meanwhile, the workplace could be completely transformed by virtual reality. People could all stay home. Wearing their virtual reality suits, they could work together in a global cyberspace community, with real and virtual colleagues. The virtual reality technology could provide the necessary controls to simply program out any "undesirable" behaviour and add in stimulating virtual interaction. An enjoyable and efficient workplace – no commuting time, less pollution from all those cars, no harassment. What an appealing alternative – and a simple technological solution to our increasingly strident gender strife! Combine this with genetically engineered babies, programmed to conform to the "parent's" specifications, and you even have an attractive alternative to marriage.

In reality, however, these virtual communities of work and personal life, which we would likely welcome as "progress," would completely imprison people's whole experience in a world of programmed human interaction. Even with the Walkman, one sees how consciousness can be imprisoned – people wearing them as they walk on a busy city street are often lost in their own worlds, totally oblivious to what's going on around them. And virtual reality would imprison all our senses, rather than just our hearing.

Who's At Home?

Is there already evidence of incarnation difficulties caused by such developments? Although I have not yet fully researched this question, the increasingly prevalent psychological phenomena of dissociative disorders seem to provide an example. These result in a person slowly detaching – dissociating – from their own experiences and their own life. The individuality can no longer "break through" – it ceases to be an active participant in its unfolding destiny.

One particularly poignant form of dissociation is Dissociative Identity Disorder (formerly known as Multiple Personality Disorder). All of us have different, often contradictory, elements of our character, which can appear at different times and in different situations. For most of us, however, these different character elements have a cohesive factor – our individuality. The bystander experiences each of these elements as different sides of the personality: the patient, considerate Lisa and the angry Lisa. Imagine that the unifying individuality withdraws, so each of the conflicting elements of the personality then appears as a distinct personality of its own, unrelated to the others. In the twinkling of an eye, the patient, considerate Ivan becomes the angry James, who has no memory of just having "been" Ivan. This disorienting and frightening condition is Dissociative Identity Disorder. Ivan's voice – and even handwriting – may be totally different from James'. The experience is not only disorienting and frightening for the person involved. It is so real and powerful that those around them can also lose their sense of what and who is real and what and who is not. It then becomes difficult to maintain one's own identity.

A commonly identified cause of such dissociative disorders is childhood trauma such as abuse, as is documented in the American Psychiatric Association's *Diagnostic and*

Statistical Manual of Mental Disorders (DSM-IV) and its associated *Study Guide to DSM-IV*, for example.[10] Grossman, however, seems to have put his finger on another type of cause when be observes that the army's desensitization program, which *intentionally* dissociated the cadets from their own experiences, has now been embraced by society as a whole. In contrast to causes of dissociation connected with specific events, this other significant cause is the steady but pervasive pollution of the human ecology through the many dehumanizing aspects of modern society. These causes, most of which are considered very acceptable elements of our society, slowly render the "home" the individuality has created for itself uninhabitable for that individuality.

Will I Use Genetically Engineered Drugs?

Let's move on. Unfortunately, it's out of the frying pan into the fire. From the dismal descriptions of the dehumanization process – making the "home" uninhabitable – to the daunting challenge: *What can I do about it?* We may decry research in fields such as cloning. But the fact is, research and manipulation of this kind will certainly continue. And forming a fruitful, individual relation to such research – and its results – is *extremely difficult.*

Craig Holdrege, author of *Genetics and the Manipulation of Life*, once put his finger on the heart of the problem – with a challenging suggestion.[11] He described the well-known experiment in which DNA from a firefly was spliced to the DNA of a tobacco plant; the resulting plant then glowed in the dark! *Are such experiments justified?* he asked. It's easy (and relatively insignificant) to dismiss such research. More fruitful, he suggested, is to imagine yourself in the following situation where you cannot be an armchair philosopher. Your beloved

Stella is likely to die if she doesn't receive a genetically engineered medication – it's the only available treatment. The decision whether or not to use the drug rests entirely on your shoulders. How will you decide?

Your initial reaction will probably be: *I don't want to use these drugs* or: *I really don't want her to die*. Understandable though they both are, neither of these judgments may have any basis in reality. Her death, for example, may be her right next step in life, however hard it would be for her friends. Holdrege then formulated a powerful criterion for making a responsible judgment: The glowing-in-the-dark tobacco plant would be justified if the new form of the tobacco plant were in keeping with the "tobacconess" of the plant. The corresponding issue to resolve with the medical treatments is: *Will using the drug support Stella's ongoing ability to unfold her "Stellaness" in the new life the drug offers her?*

When treatment offers mere life support, "life as a vegetable," where only a shadow of the person comes to expression, this question may be relatively easy to answer. But with genetically engineered drugs, kidney dialysis or chemotherapy, which offer the person a "new life," the questions are far more complicated.

At the heart of the question of Stella being able to continue to unfold her "Stellaness" or the genetically engineered tobacco plant its "tobacconess" stands a *major* problem: most of us cannot see either Stella's "Stellaness" or the tobacco plant's "tobacconess." And, lacking the capacities needed to see these, our judgments about such questions will not be founded in reality.

This is a humbling fact to recognize. We are like people who haven't learned anatomy and physiology being assigned to perform brain surgery. Unfortunately, the implications of this realization are vast. Because it is life that has assigned us the job. We need to be ready, but aren't. Using biblical imagery, we've arrived at the wedding but are not dressed for the occasion.

Seeing My Neighbour As I See Myself

How can I see Stella's "Stellaness"? First and foremost, I must learn how to get *inside her experience*. To illustrate this, let's look at how other people see us. Each of us is painfully aware of the extent to which others can see merely the external aspects, the "surface" of who I really am. They know my daughter's a lawyer, that my son's just gotten married, and that I'm a carpenter. Perhaps they know my parents were Spanish and that my mother had been killed in an accident. They know how big my house is, speculate about how affluent I am and have some idea of my construction skills. And, of course, they all know really well what's wrong with my character. But few of them even begin to see more deeply into who I really am. Or synthesize these external facts into a comprehensive view of me as a whole person.

Thomas Weihs, author of *Children in Need of Special Care* and one of the founders of the Camphill Movement for the care of individuals with handicaps, once came up with a helpful insight into what it means to get inside another person's experience. He was elucidating the biblical dictum *Love your neighbour as yourself.*[12] Looking at my neighbour, says Weihs, I see some isolated facts about the "surface" of who she is (ethnic background, job, family, etc., factors of the type just enumerated). But these are like an album of unrelated, individual photographs of discrete aspects of her life, taken at discrete times. By contrast, the way I know myself is completely different. None of these discrete facts is isolated for me. I always experience them as a part of the totality that I call myself. This totality also exists in time – my last year's painful divorce experiences are part of who I am today. I see myself within the moving, continuous totality of the drama that is my life and myself. Using a somewhat trivial analogy, I experience myself as if in a "life movie-drama," in contrast to the unrelated collection of "photo album shots" of my neighbour. Or, to use another image, it is like dancing under a strobe-light: with my own dancing, I experience from within its totality and fullness of movement. But for other peoples' *movement*, I am a half-blind onlooker. I see only the discrete, static poses their dancing leaves in the successive strobe-light moments. The movements themselves I cannot see.

Hence, when I see my neighbour being nasty to a colleague, I generally can't see the "movement" around the event. So I think: *She's got a problem!* But when I'm equally nasty to a colleague, it's certainly not because *I* have a problem. It's because one of my kids is sick and I didn't sleep last night. Because of the way I see my neighbour, says Weihs, I don't love – or forgive – my neighbour. Because of the way I *see* myself, I tend to love – and forgive – myself. To love my neighbour as myself requires me to learn to see my neighbour the way I *see* myself. To get beyond my strobe-light experience, and get inside the movement of her experience.

The capacity to get inside the world that's outside me, to experience the "inside of the outside" in an active and mobile way, is a gift young children possess naturally. They actively get inside things. Their sense impressions are merely the wide-open doorways for their active, mobile experience of the inside of the world around them. Notice sometime how perceptive a young child can be of someone he has never met before, getting inside the person's voice, gestures, mood and facial expressions. He does not just passively "spectate." He imitates – gets inside that experience and then actively *does* what he sees.

As the child grows older, these wide-open doorways slowly close shut – he joins the onlooker world we adults inhabit. The young child, curious, full of wonder, is on the other side of that doorway in a flash – whether it's a physical doorway or the doorway of their sense impressions. We adults, by contrast, tend to look passively at the doorway, reluctant to make the effort to go through it. Meanwhile, we construct armchair theories about what's on the other side.

Practise! Practise! Practise!

Weihs' insight shows *where* we need to go. Back through that doorway. Inside my neighbour's experience. So I actively see her in the way I see myself, within a moving, integrated life-drama.

The question is: *How* do I get there?

Try this exercise some time: Choose a person you know well. Take different aspects of her life and try to form them into a cohesive and mobile drama. See if you can allow one image from her life to develop into the next, as you could for yourself. Write it down, perhaps – as beautifully as possible. Or try to draw her face. Or imitate or sketch her body gesture. (The end result is totally unimportant; it's the activity that counts. It's like playing basketball regularly; the number of baskets you make is secondary to the activity). You are trying to discover her "story," as Oliver Sacks describes so beautifully in *A Matter of Identity* (a case-study in *The Man who Mistook his Wife for a Hat* about a patient who had lost his memory through a severe illness):

> *If we wish to know about a [person], we ask 'what is his story - his real inmost story?' – for each of us is a biography, a story. Each of us* is *a singular narrative....*

Through the exercise, you are trying to tell her flowing,

integrated narrative, as a good biographer would, in a way that reveals the individuality who is its real "author." Through telling his patients' stories, rather than merely describing their clinical histories, Sacks himself has developed a remarkable ability to see – or at least glimpse – the individualities of his patients, the real "writers" of his stories:

> *To be ourselves, we must have ourselves – possess ... our life-stories. We must 'recollect' ourselves, recollect the inner drama, the narrative of ourselves.*[13]

Possessing the other person's life-story, recollecting her inner drama, actively getting inside her experience in a mobile way, means learning to glimpse – and eventually see – her "Stellaness."

Rudolf Steiner suggested a similar exercise to help develop the capacity to see the "tobacconess" of a plant.[14] Take a plant you know well, a melon, perhaps. First, look very carefully at its seed. Then visualize its initial, green, sprouting leaves. Then follow its prolific, tentacle-like growth through its yellow-orange blossoms and abundant, juicy fruit. See if you can recreate this growth in your own mind as a continuous process. If you can manage this, you slowly learn to get inside what makes it grow as it does – its "melonness."

Through making such efforts, we can slowly learn to leave our passive, onlooker world and go back consciously through that doorway, to experience knowledge again in the active, lively and mobile way we did as children – but now consciously.

Trying these exercises can be humbling, however. You may find you don't have the concentration to do them, even for a few minutes. And if you do have enough concentration, you'll find how difficult it is to allow the images to unfold in continuous development, the way the plant itself grows or the person's life develops. All consciousness transformation takes immense effort. Think how much effort it took you to learn to think scientifically. Remember the years-long effort you had to go through just to learn mathematics. What is 4 x 23? What is 23.65% of the difference between 4,989.4 and 423.985? What is $55x^4y^3 \div 13x^3y^5$. Solve the simultaneous quadratic equations $13x^2-5y^2=7$, $7x^2+5y^2=73$, etc., etc., etc. Aren't you glad those days are over? Each of us spent years of our lives going through this agony. This individual learning process is the one humanity as a whole underwent during the Renaissance, in order to transform our Middle Ages consciousness into our modern one. If we are to confront the Brave New World challenges posed by life today, we will have to undergo a similarly rigorous, individual transformation. Only a new renaissance of radical consciousness transformation, as fundamental as that of the last Renaissance, can bring about the urgent changes needed today.

Are these faculties attainable for us regular mortals? They certainly are. Some years ago, I had a friend who decided to learn a musical instrument. He was almost thirty and, as far as I know, had no unusual musical gifts and had not learned an instrument as a child. Yet, within a few years, he became a very proficient flautist. What was the secret? I'm sure many of you know the story of the person, violin in hand, walking up New York's Fifth Avenue and asking a passerby for directions: *How do I get to Carnegie Hall?* she asked. *Practise! Practise! Practise!* came the wise answer.

At the Grave Of Civilization

Anyone who's willing to put forth the effort can learn an instrument, become proficient in calculus, or develop the faculties I am describing. Clearly, how far each individual can go depends on their individual destiny. My friend will probably not become a Jean-Pierre Rampal, nor will the person who takes up physics at age thirty likely become the next Albert Einstein. Likewise, those who regularly undertake such exercises will probably not become the next Rudolf Steiner. Frankly, that's not the issue. In our increasingly dehumanized world, developing the eyes to perceive destiny is a crucial faculty. It becomes ever more urgent that we learn to get at least a glimpse, a sense, of our neighbour's "Stellaness." This is the "seed" from which her life is growing – in the sense of Sacks' statement that "each of us *is* a biography." It is the fruit of her previous lives, which she brought with her through birth. With persistent practice, our glimpses – learning to gently and sensitively "touch" her destiny – can slowly evolve towards vision.

At the same time, our Brave New World confronts us with an increasingly dehumanizing technological and social onslaught – and generally, we have little idea how much the prison doors of our Brave New World Technostructure have already closed (with humanity on the inside). What the world desperately needs is "architects," people who understand "building," people who know, through having developed the necessary faculties, how the Technostructure is being constructed as a Brave New World prison. Using the same faculties, these "architects" can contribute to the building of another, greater-than-human structure (in contrast to the less-than-human Technostructure). In my book, *Mephistopheles' Anvil*, I call this building the Temple of Humanity.

Every new mechanistic development, each building stone for the Technostructure, directly challenges our ability to see. Do we have the capacities to distinguish whether the glowing-in-the-dark tobacco plant retains its "tobacconess?" Or to know Stella's "Stellaness" well enough to be able to make responsible decisions about genetically engineered drugs? Can we discern what is happening when a personality withdraws (in dissociation conditions, for example)? Without these faculties of seeing, we will be completely blind to what stands before us in these ever more powerful challenges. We will then be at the mercy of the forces that drive us further into our Brave New World imprisonment.

It is, of course, each individual's choice whether to become an "architect" of this kind or to stay as a person who is content to be swept along by the tide. But, just as every conventional architect is *required* to learn mathematics, anyone who decides to become one of these "architects" *has* to develop new faculties of seeing. Holdrege's challenge shows how the capacity needed to confront the issues of cloning is the same as the faculty needed to perceive how the fruits of a person's previous incarnation manifest in this incarnation. This is the way all such technological developments work. They are not merely evil. Each new development confronts us with a challenge: either we develop these new faculties or we'll be swept along, unconscious of what is being done to us and the rest of humanity. And woe to us if we don't heed this challenge. We will soon find that humanity is already at the "grave of civilization," to use Rudolf Steiner's phrase.[15]

We can only develop the spiritual faculties we need for our future evolution through confronting these challenges head-on. Mephistopheles says of himself in Goethe's *Faust: [I am] a part of that power / That ever would the evil do / But ever does the good.*[16] Mephistopheles provides us with an anvil. Only through striking our hammer against this anvil – with the help of fire – can we forge the new faculties we need for the future. The immense danger each of us faces, of course, is that I may be paralyzed – that my spirit may be severely burned or broken – through the intense fire and the powerful impact of my hammer against the anvil of evil.

Communism provided such an anvil for the dissidents of

Eastern Europe. The evils of the racial hatred and injustice provided a similar anvil for Martin Luther King. On their anvils of evil these outstanding individualities developed new spiritual faculties. Cloning and all our other Brave New World developments provide a similar Mephistophelean anvil against which all of us in Western societies will forge our new faculties – or become paralyzed, with broken spirits.

If we want to be "architects" of the kind I have described, it is irresponsible within the urgency of today's world to "modestly" say: *Developing such faculties will take me many incarnations.* Cloning research and the like will not wait for our modesty. They press on us the urgency to develop these essential capacities *now.* Otherwise, our inactivity makes us *directly co-responsible* for such developments.

As we stand at the grave of civilization, are we willing to be thrown into prison, face the fire hoses, or do whatever the modern Western equivalent is? Or even just do the hard, disciplined and rigorous work it takes to energetically practise "simple" exercises like those described above – again and again and again? This practice is far more important – and far more difficult – than reading lecture after lecture or going to endless meetings where people "share what's on their hearts" (which, unfortunately, is often whatever just happens to breeze through their heads).

Note that the wise New Yorker did not say: *Go to meetings about music and Discuss! Discuss! Discuss!* Or: *Read Lectures! Lectures! Lectures! about music*. He said: *Practise! Practise! Practise! Practise!*

That's what my flautist friend understood and *did.*

It works.

And it's a matter of life or death: Will I help build the Temple of Humanity – or contribute to the Brave New World Technostructure?

References

[1] Huxley, Aldous, *Brave New World and Brave New World Revisited*, NewYork, Harper Perennial, 1998. Pages 2-3 of *Brave New World Revisited.*

[2] Huxley, Aldous, op. cit., page 4 of *Brave New World Revisited.*

[3] *New York Times*, November 3, 1993, page A16 (the British murder). *Philadelphia Inquirer*, March 26, 1998, page A1, A20 (the Jonesboro, AK murder).

[4] Healy, Jane M., *Endangered Minds: Why Children Don't Think and What We Can Do About It,* New York, Simon and Schuster, 1990.

[5] Grossman, Dave, *On Killing: The Psychological Cost of Learning to Kill in War and Society,* New York, Little Brown and Company, 1995, especially pages 3, 89 29, 35, 251, 307-311.

[6] Alexandra, John, *Mephistopheles' Anvil: Forging a More Human Future,* Spring Valley, NY, Rose Harmony Publications, 1996.

[7] *Wall Street Journal,* July 23, 1998, pages B1, B7.

[8] *Newsweek,* March 10, 1997, pages 53-59.

[9] Rheingold, Howard, *Virtual Reality,* New York, Summit Books, 1991, especially Chapter 16.

[10] *Diagnostic and Statistical Manual of Mental Disorders* (DSM-IV) and Fauman, Michael A., *Study Guide to DSM-IV,* Washington, American Psychiatric Association, 1994. *Manual* pages 484-487, *Study Guide* page 267 282.

[11] Holdrege, Craig, *Genetics and the Manipulation of Life: The Forgotten Factor of Context,* Hudson, NY, Lindisfarne Press, 1996. The British edition is entitled: *A Question of Genes,* Edinburgh, Floris Books, 1996. The observation cited was mentioned in a lecture in Chestnut Ridge, NY, on March 18, 1996.

[12] Thomas Weihs made this observation at an international conference in Krefeld, Germany in July, 1969. The photo album, movie and strobe-light images are my elaboration of his essential insight.

[13] Sacks, Oliver, *The Man who Mistook his Wife for a Hat,* New York, Harper Perennial, 1990, pages 110-111.

[14] Rudolf Steiner, *How to Know Higher Worlds: A Modern Path of Initiation,* Hudson, NY, Anthroposophic Press, 1994, pages 56-57.

[15] Rudolf Steiner, *Karmic Relationships,* Volume VI, London, Rudolf Steiner Press, 1983, page 163.

[16] Goethe, J.W. v., *Faust, Parts 1 & 2,* translated by George Madison Priest, New York, Alfred A. Knopf, 1969, *Part I,* lines 1336-7.

The Biodynamic Farm: an Embryo for the Threefold Social Order in our Time

Manfred Klett

This title might well seem to exaggerate the importance of agriculture. After all, does it not appear to be in a miserable state and, in terms of economics, as a secondary issue or simply a nuisance, absorbing as it does increasing amounts of subsidies to the detriment of our natural environment? This is true, but is this not the clearest indication that farming as a cultural task has finally died, and does not this death present opportunities that we can as yet scarcely imagine? The demise of agriculture in the Christian West was complete by the beginning of the sixties. Ever since it has been a victim of industry ending up in this miserable state carrying out what science, technology, politics and the world market force it to do.

The fate of the threefold social order and the death of agriculture

It is worthwhile recalling the years from 1917 to 1922, when Rudolf Steiner boldly tried to cultivate a consciousness of and to establish the threefold social order in Central Europe in the chaotic years following the first World War. He looked for support among the working classes, the uprooted people who had lost their traditional background in the course of the nineteenth century and whose urgent questions about their future lives remained unanswered. They were the true representatives of the "social question". In those days after World War I, farmers still made up 40% of the working population (today the figure is 3%), and preserved their traditional way of life. The church was still alive in most villages, the individual still unquestionably served the community. In spite of the great efforts and the deep devotion which were invested by so many people to bring the threefold social order into being, one has to acknowledge that the endeavour failed. Aside from the hyper-inflation of the 1920s, there was one overriding reason: our consciousness was not up to it.

Has this changed at all since then? For decades valuable works on the social question have been published, and some attempts have been made to put them into practice. But somehow they have remained incomplete, they have not been strong enough to radiate into and to restructure social life. One basic element that could not be taken hold of was the economic life, and today's global economy is completely beyond control.

Meanwhile, unnoticed in a hidden, neglected niche of social life as it were, the death of agriculture took place. With it went any semblance of an ideal world one could withdraw to. The social question now faces the environmental question. Agriculture is no longer a matter of inheritance, nor can it be seen as the bearer of the folk soul. Its death means that it has been released from the age of the intellectual soul and now needs to be reborn into the age of the consciousness soul. Its rebirth means biodynamic farming.

Death reveals what life conceals. In face of the ruins left by industrialisation − manipulative applied science, strangling legislation, short-term economics − we are forced to grasp the idea of agriculture anew and in full consciousness. In doing so and in putting it into practice we most surprisingly find that it contains two aspects of social threefoldness which relate to one another, like a seed containing two cotyledons.

The essence of biodynamic farming in relation to man

What is the essence of biodynamic farming, which penetrates as deeply into nature as it does into social life in an evolutionary process leading far into the future? Agriculture is like a skin, where social life meets the life of the Earth and where they interpenetrate (see sketch). Each farm may be seen as a cell of this skin which itself is revealed in the cultivated landscape.

If we now put ourselves in the position of somebody who has grown up in London or in eastern Europe beyond the former iron curtain and we assume the person concerned has internalised the spiritual concept of biodynamic farming and wants to put it into practice, we face the problem of creating something out of nothing. Where does he get the land or the capital from? Where are the like-minded people to help form a collaborative community? He has nothing but the spiritual concept of Biodynamics in mind, yet it is strong enough to move mountains. This idea as a world in itself is contained in the following words by Rudolf Steiner: "Now a farm actually fulfils its being in the best sense of the word when it can be conceived of as a kind of individuality, a real self-contained individuality". (This is an attempt at literal translation; the English and American editions of the Agricultural Course each quote a slightly different version.) Spiritual research tells us that biodynamic farming is not primarily an ecological matter but has to do with a right understanding of the human being. We are invited to learn to know ourselves as a microcosm, as an individuality which expresses itself in the threefoldness of our body. Study of the morphology and function of the human body reveals three autonomous systems which house the soul spirit with its three soul faculties.

Observing the head, it is a concentration of the nerve-sense-system. As a sphere it rests quietly on the shoulders. The skull is of crystalline bony substance enveloping the brain, which swims in the cerebral fluid. The brain substance – the foundation for our thinking – continuously tends to decay and needs a continuous flow of nourishment from the blood. In our head everything is closer to death than to life.

Looking at our limbs and our metabolism, we encounter a system which is the polar opposite. The limbs radiate into the world. Everything is alive and in a state of conscious or unconscious movement, an expression of our will.

As an independent realm and yet mediating between the two poles, we find the rhythmic or circulatory system in the breathing lungs and the beating heart. These rhythmic organs are sheltered by the thorax, which is closed towards the head, half open in its own sphere by the sequence of the ribs and fully open towards the stomach, separated only by the diaphragm. In this realm our feeling manifests.

These three systems interrelate and form the human body as a "self-contained individuality". It is a microcosm, comprising as an image the wholeness of the macrocosm. In observing ourselves we can find what is needed to educate and develop ourselves and, hence, what is needed to educate and develop the Earth into the future. Referring to his Agricultural Course, Rudolf Steiner observes: "Everywhere the starting point is the study of man, man will be the foundation".

The threefoldness of the farm individuality

But how do we find our way from man to nature? The answer to this question leads to a rebirth of agriculture. Imagine standing in a field on a midsummer day, observing the ripening rye. The soil is hard and dry. Invisibly, the roots submerge into the darkness of the solid earth, oriented towards the centre of the Earth, splitting off into the tiny root hairs, almost fusing with the crystalline minerals, enhancing the process of weathering and sensing the salty substances that are dissolved and thus absorbing them. Beneath our feet, reaching into the far depths of the Earth, rests the mineral world, crystalline, motionless, solid, progressively decaying, everything closer to death than to life, and like silica a reflector and earthly sense organ of the formative forces of the distant heavens. The geological foundation below our feet is the head pole of the agricultural individuality.

Above the soil, our view rests upon an abundance of ever changing phenomena. The wind sends silver waves rippling over the rye field. After a spell of bright sunshine, a thunderstorm pours heavy showers over the land, nothing stays the same for even a moment. In all weathers everything is alive and in motion. We look into and live in the belly, the metabolic pole of this individuality, which, compared with a human being, stands upright on its head, linking Earth and Sun.

Where these two poles meet and interact, a thin inconspicuous skinlike layer manifests: the soil. Rudolf Steiner calls it the diaphragm of the agricultural individuality. From this skin, all plant life shoots up year after year, materialising as an image this invisible vertical axis of directive forces between earth and sun. The term "diaphragm" is well chosen to characterise the soil. Both neither breathe nor pulsate by themselves. They merely react to the forces from above and beneath. But as the diaphragm has the potential actively to enhance the breathing of the lungs, the soil is able actively to maintain and provide fertility.

Thus the task of a reborn agriculture is to educate and develop this capacity and to enliven the solid earth which thus becomes an ever more independent and autonomous realm between the two poles of the heights and the depths.

All agricultural work must serve this task. The most effective educational means "to fulfil the being of the farm individuality" are the different fertilisers deriving from plant (humus), animal (manure) and man (biodynamic preparations). Humus and manure are fertilisers nature provides. They enliven the soil in the horizontal dimension in a more universal sense. The biodynamic preparations, however, are the result of a technology deriving from spiritual research. They come about through a free human deed and by devotion to their spiritual origin. They are new substances, introduce individualising forces into nature and thus work vertically, developing and strengthening the threefoldness. The horn-manure preparation for example relates to the plant root, a "head fertiliser"; the horn-silica preparation is a fertiliser of the metabolism relating to plant growth; while the compost preparations enliven the soil as such, strengthening its mediating function.

A self-contained farm involves building a body, an organism, in the horizontal for this vertically oriented individuality. In linking together the mineral, plant and animal kingdom on a higher stage, it should provide all the means not only to sustain soil fertility, but to transform and enliven earthly matter.

Biodynamic farming extending into social life

The task of biodynamic farming points to a future evolution of the Earth: it is nothing less than planting into nature and the work of the past the idea of development. Can this tremendous task ever be performed by those tragic few who are left to steer machines for the sake of maximising turnover, or by those happy few who have grasped the idea of biodynamic farming? It is impossible. It was possible as long as social welfare was still inherent in agriculture. But through its death it has become part of the general social scene of present civilisation. It is for this reason that biodynamic farming, being the answer to the environmental question, offers a tremendous creative power to help to answer the social question. It expands from year to year beyond the limits of the farm, deeper into the life of the civilisation around it. This often means a double burden for the people on the farms, and in many places the social bridge-building is more challenging than the biodynamic work itself. It is symptomatic of the dependence upon the social life around that because of its ever growing complexity there is no area left where the biodynamic farmer or gardener can solve his problems alone. He is dependent for better or for worse at all levels on the energy and consciousness, the capacities and the collaboration of people who are not directly involved in agriculture. On the other hand it is equally symptomatic that biodynamic farming offers the task of taking responsibility for the Earth which is beneficial to the whole of society.

Since the final industrialisation of agriculture in the sixties, a new awareness of the environment has arisen in society. But in general, it has no real goal. The objective is nature conservancy and the avoidance of further destruction. As soon as people come into contact with the broader vision of biodynamic farming, they realise that there is something as yet unknown which calls for an inner change, the commitment to turn from passive observation to the active shaping of social processes. What is the objective of this creative shaping? It is again a threefold one, the second cotyledon in the one seed capsule.

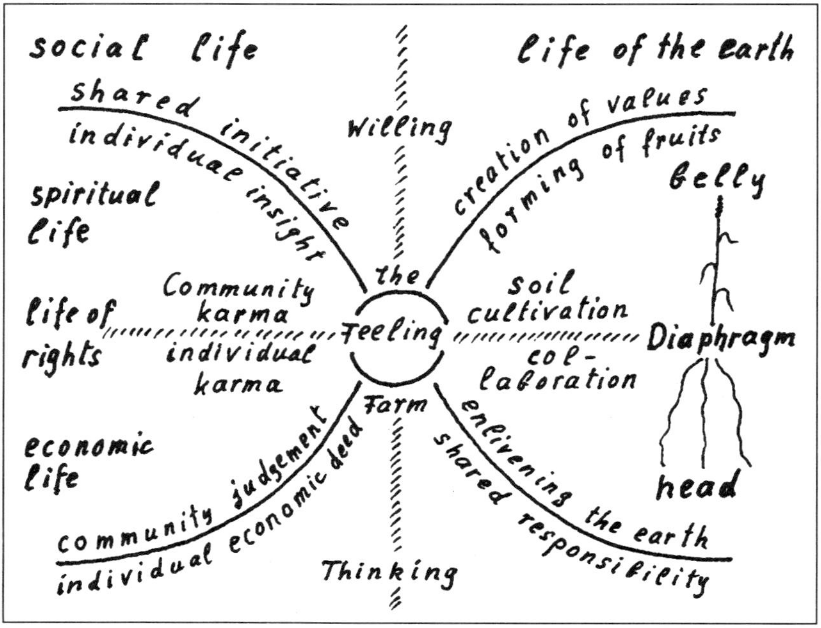

Agriculture as the forming mediator between social life and life of the earth

Shaping social life in the spiritual sphere

Let us imagine a biodynamic farmer's family or rather a collaborating community of farmers. They do the work, plough the field, feed the cows, care for the seed, make the preparations, plant hedges and everything else. They are dealing with a universe, condensed into a farm organism. It affords a tremendous amount of knowledge, not academic, but spiritual knowledge which rationally penetrates every detail of the physical, living and intellectual realm, and which really is capable of overcoming the abyss between ourselves and the spiritual reality which remains hidden from our senses. In biodynamic farming, we encounter the germ for a renewal of spiritual life altogether. But this is now not one of further emancipation from nature, by which we achieved freedom and self-consciousness. That we have already achieved. Now is the time to take free initiative and responsibility to support the active farmers with insights and individual abilities. If we imagine the concept of the farm individuality becoming alive in ever more people's minds, they would joyfully contribute their ideas and put their abilities at the farm's service. This is already happening in many places. Moreover this increasingly enables the biodynamic farmer to answer the questions of an ignorant but interested public out of his own actual experience. The content of the Agricultural Course has so far proved difficult to transmit in the form of ideas. Thus circles of friends are increasingly forming around the farms; communities that share initiative, responsibility and skills. It is not only the people on the farms who find themselves with an educational task of a new sort, but the whole farm itself becomes an open centre for learning. A new and altruistic spiritual life – one of active initiative – is igniting around biodynamic farms. When people from outside take on shared responsibility for the farm, consciousness expands over this bit of the earth, and interest awakens from person to person, something that can ripen to morally effective conviction.

There are members of such social support groups who might even join in the practical work, caring for the hedges, the birds, and offering whatever help is needed. Others are more inclined to participate in farm research and training and in study work with the farmers or in arranging seasonal celebrations. Yet the main emphasis should be put on the working with the preparations. All free initiative should focus on this future task to enliven the head function of the farm individuality.

It is inherent in the spiritual dimension of biodynamic farming that research and training finds its appropriate place within the organism of the farm individuality. The practical work can not be done without a research attitude. The farmer needs help in developing this. Unlimited questions are waiting to be worked on, and everybody is invited to offer his skills. The complementary gesture is a growing willingness to collaborate between the biodynamic farmers and research institutes at universities.

Another great enrichment, but also a challenge from the spiritual cultural point of view, is collaboration with people from other fields of work. Biodynamic farms become crystallisation points, local centres, inspiring other activities such as baking, cheese making, running a farm-shop, making handicrafts, or providing curative education, social therapy or even just normal schooling. When this is the case, a new social awareness can spread. Social arrangements become more flexible and innovative.

The social environment starts to correspond to the farm or farms, and new spiritual life germinates and unites people not merely out of sympathy but through spiritual interest. On the social front, free initiative, ideas and skills start to be shared. The metabolic pole of the social organism, the cultural spiritual sphere, is stirred up, re-enlivened and intensified, while establishing forms of agriculture by entrepreneurial means that would take shape from these enlivened ideas. The metabolic pole of the social organism nourishes the head pole of the farm individuality.

Shaping social life in the economic sphere

Let us now imagine the farmer who starts to harvest the rye or whatever crops have ripened. The greater the variety of cultivated crops and animal husbandry, the healthier and more self-contained the farm organism. Both metabolic poles, the spiritual life of the social organism and the spiritual life of the farm individuality, bring forth a spiritual output on different levels. On the one side, initiative, skills, ideas; on the other fruit formation. On the social side there is a need for the ripened fruit. The latter is transformed into a product once it leaves the farm organism and enters economic life. When it passes the threshold, its objective value, which derives from the natural conditions of its farm origin, is also transformed into an economic value. Both values should ideally be comparable, though at present they are far apart.

It is at the threshold between the metabolic area of the farm and the economic life that the prime productivity occurs, the creation of value from which all economics, also industrial goods, should take their measure. The economic life consists of production, distribution and consumption. These three functions are closely linked. From the point of view of quality, freshness, costs of transport and so on, the distance from the farm to the consumer should be as short as possible. Thus the regional market is most appropriate for biodynamic agriculture − exactly the opposite of what is currently described as an agricultural world market.

Biodynamic prime production provides a unique opportunity to build up local markets on an associative basis. Contrary to current economic behaviour in general, measures can be taken there to exclude egoism and make agriculture the needle on the scale where a new form of shared welfare is emerging. And in fact we see on all sides quiet attempts at bridge building to neighbouring farms, to the processors, distributors and consumers. This is reflected in agreements as to what is planted to cover actual needs, in the founding of and co-operating with decentralised processing enterprises on or near the farms. In distribution, the same route of decentralisation is followed. The spectrum stretches from the farm shop with special forms of direct purchase as in "community supported gardening or agriculture" – widely developed in the US – and vegetable crate-subscription systems via the regional distributors on to wholesalers.

The incipient regional market shows every sign of becoming the starting point for economic associations. In forming such markets, the ambivalent mass of consumers can be educated into becoming dependable economic partners. An increasing number of them can be won over as active co-shapers of the economic process. Thus consumer egotism can be transformed into genuine interest in the individual economic partner and in particular in the goals of biodynamic farming.

Starting out from agriculture, the associative principle can be exercised here and now in eradicating competition and in practising collaboration in the sense of brotherhood. Associations can only grow up where strict account is taken of the given state of consciousness among their partners, in direct face to face meetings, in immediate contact with the economic facts and in the schooling of practical thinking on the basis of these facts. Symptoms of our time indicate that from now on, economic associations are growing and must grow out of the "regionality" of agriculture. Biodynamic farming is called upon by the spirit of the age to moderate the excesses of economics and to transform present economic thinking.

The task of such associations is clearly delineated in forming "round tables", where the economic partners of a region meet and discuss how to satisfy the region's needs, how to arrive at a "just price" and what investments or debt-settlements are needed. Thus the associations deriving from biodynamic farming serve the social organism as its organ of perception and thinking. It generates true social judgements, community judgements. It can make adjustments at root level before abuses appear, that can then only be checked by abstract laws and the controls that follow. If the economic life is to prosper in a human way, it must be composed of interrelating associations which may start from agriculture and eventually seek connections to industry. If we consider the function of economic associations, we can understand that economic life is the head of the social organism, the counter-pole to spiritual life.

Shaping social life in the rights sphere

We have now polarised the spiritual life and economic life of the social organism against the background of the farm individuality. In the latter, we discovered a mediating realm, the soil, which comes to life when we fertilise it. In the social organism, the sphere of rights is the mediating barren or fertile realm which corresponds to the barren or fertile soil. This also needs to be fertilised. This happens when we raise the relation between the life of rights and the life of the developing "diaphragm" to consciousness. We might then feel that there is an unresolved question about ownership. If we deal with this question, we might eventually achieve the capacity to be able to separate ourselves with our karma from the stream of heredity, to become independent of any attachment to property. Thus we establish the possibility of entering into new forms of collaboration with others as equals among equals. As these relationships arise, the rights life receives further fructification from the agricultural individuality by the creation of a new community karma which frees itself from all bondage to a territory, race or nation.

The main challenge to build this new community karma

is to overcome the defined rights that limit the future. Not least because relations between people can remain anonymous. What is urgently needed – and this is something which ought to be fertilised by free initiatives from above and by community judgements of real brotherhood from below – is rights based on trust and on the feeling of justice that arise among people like plants rise from the soil. Trust as a substance of rights emerges when a group of people is constantly at work, testing, maintaining and developing the sense of rights in their practical application. The right to use the farm land and working capital or, rather, the right to operate the "farm individuality" – without payment of rent – is a touchstone for whether a legal community is strong enough to rely on trust. The right to own and run a farm is normally handed over by inheritance, purchase or lease. Here the old notions of rights prevail. If we take seriously the idea that the land, or better still the whole of the farm individuality, cannot be a commodity, i.e. not to be purchased or sold, then it is subject only to an autonomous rights relationship. The right of ownership than dissolves into a body of persons extending beyond the bounds of the farm. They act in the sphere of spiritual life and will out of shared responsibility guard the right and pass it on to a new group of farmers when the time has come.

In recent decades, many attempts have been made to find new legal forms for the use of land and farm capital based on trust. They are to be found in farming communities and in "community supported farming and gardening" enterprises. Such forms in the rights sphere are based on declarations of intent that are open to the future, not fixed and tied to paragraphs. If we enter this open legal framework, rights develop in relationship to individual karma and the karma of the collaborating community. These legal forms for "practical rights" growing out of life have no place, no recognition within official legal systems. But in order to exist at all, such a rights life has to be adjusted to existing legal norms. As a rule, this takes the form of a foundation, charitable trust or civil association.

If we accept the challenge of reason and set off on the path of a "rightless sphere", that is to practise rights based on trust, then the social realm becomes full of creative possibilities for change. The operation of the farm individuality lies fully in the hands of the groups of farmers. As soon as they end their work, the right to dispose of the farm dissolves into a community which cares for the transition, replacing heredity, lease and purchase or sale.

There is another impact of biodynamic farming on the development of a living sense of rights in the social environment. It is a question of income and of how to integrate as many co-workers, apprentices and practitioners as are necessary to fully establish the farm individuality. How little this can be the concern of the individual farmer is shown in its negative aspect on the one hand by the subsidies that are poured into agriculture. On the other hand there are not sufficient means to finance urgently needed co-workers, while unemployment abounds. Direct payments are no solution to ensure income and compensate for prices that fall to world market levels. They are far from being able to finance the necessary increase in hands that must be devoted to biodynamic farming. The securing of the income can be achieved by setting prices in the economic associations in accordance with the costs from one harvest to the next.

Biodynamic farming is ready to solve the problem of unemployment. Unemployment means that there is excessive industrial activity and insufficient agricultural activity. The pendulum has swung from agriculture to industry in the past.

Now it could swing back. A renewal of education, the rights life and economic life is dependent on people finding their way back into agriculture where they are urgently needed.

The farmer between two threefold entities

If we imagine ourselves in the midst of our soul-being, standing on the border line between the life of the Earth and social life, our soul forces reach out into the inner configuration of nature and into the intimacies of social life. In each of these realms they establish in a narrower or wider context a threefolded unity: the agricultural individuality and the social organism. Both are a reflection and at the same time an expansion of our individual being and the being of a collaborating community. On both sides, thinking and willing are inverted. The spirit-will in the social sphere transforms earthly matter in order to bring about a renewed working of cosmic thought in nature. What spirit engenders in nature by forming fruits becomes the basis for holistic social thinking in the economic sphere, the "head" of the social organism. This thinking must, in exercising "common sense", see to it that everybody's needs are met. Through our feeling we weave together the sphere of rights in which karma shapes itself with the Earth's mediating realm, the soil-diaphragm. It is from this that our body takes the forces for living out our karma, and it is into this that the outcome of karma is inscribed.

Thus from the viewpoint we have taken here, the agricultural individuality and the social organism are two sides of the same coin. The one can neither exist nor develop without the other.

The Meeting of Karmic Streams in the Communications Age

Simon Blaxland-de Lange

In the course of several lectures which he gave in 1924 to members of the Anthroposophical Society, Rudolf Steiner characterised two principal groups of people whose karma would lead them to Anthroposophy in the twentieth century, namely, the Platonists and the Aristotelians. He also emphasised – and this gives the present article its cue – the great importance of these two karmic streams finding their way to one another and actively collaborating at the end of the present century. It is no part of the purpose of this article to reformulate the characterisations which Rudolf Steiner gave of these two streams, not least because this is a complex field of study in itself. Fortunately, this task has already been thoroughly carried out by the Dutch historian and teacher, Hans Peter van Manen, whose book *Christussucher und Michaeldiener* (1980)[1] formed the main content of the 1990 Summer Conference of the Anthroposophical Society in Great Britain. However, readers who are not directly familiar with these descriptions may find in what follows a possible path towards understanding the underlying themes.

As van Manen implies in his book, this is a theme whose significance extends far beyond the limited confines of the Anthroposophical Society. While it would be thoroughly misleading to suggest that the terms are synonymous, it could be said with some justice that the two principal karmic streams of the Anthroposophical Society are representative in microcosmic form of the two great streams of consciousness out of which Christianity came into being, the so-called "Kings" and "Shepherds";[2] and there is ultimately also – though here it is more a matter of proposing an analogy than suggesting an equivalence – in a certain sense a relationship with the two ancient streams of mankind, those of Abel/Seth and Cain, or Solomon and Hiram. To the extent that the dichotomy between Platonists and Aristotelians is symptomatic of polarities of various kinds between wider groups of human beings, a genuine meeting between these groups within the Anthroposophical Society at the end of the present century must inevitably have significance also for these wider circles of humanity, as a means of bringing healing in many areas where there is now misunderstanding and strife. On the other hand, these wider divisions, by the same token, represent obstacles to such a meeting taking place within the Anthroposophical Society at the present time. The purpose of this article is to offer a tentative appraisal of the present relationship between these karmic streams within the Anthroposophical Society, how the imbalance between the two might be rectified and what the result might look like.[3] This appraisal will now be introduced by setting it in a wider context of cultural and social evolution.

Shortly after the end of the First World War, Rudolf Steiner gave two series of lectures in Dornach to an audience including a group of members of the Anthroposophical Society in England, the first between 12th and 15th December 1919 and the second between 20th and 22nd February 1920.[4] The relevance of these lectures to the present theme is that they enable a late twentieth century reader to gain some inkling of the spiritual forces underlying present social and cultural phenomena and, hence, to begin to make some sense of them.

What Rudolf Steiner presents in these lectures is essentially a picture of the post-Atlantean cultural period as it has hitherto unfolded; but instead of describing it – as elsewhere – as a series of five cultural epochs, he characterises three distinct cultural elements, or "mysteries", which have in very different ways carried or guided the process of historical (and prehistorical) development since Atlantis. These three elements are the Mysteries of Spirit or Light, which have their origin in oriental wisdom and are associated with theocracy, or the unquestioned rulership of the divine on Earth; the Mysteries of Space, where this spiritual authority is no longer experienced directly but as vested in an earthly representative such as an emperor or king (whether this be an Egyptian Pharaoh, a Roman Emperor, a pope or king); and the Mysteries of Earth, which have come into ascendancy only in the last two or three centuries through the democratic individualism of the Anglo-American West. Each of these "mysteries" has a particular relationship to one sphere of the threefold social organism – respectively, the spiritual-cultural sphere, the sphere of rights, and the economic sphere.

In focussing upon the present phase of dominance of the Anglo-American West, Rudolf Steiner's main thrust is to underline the centrality of the economic sphere and to dismiss any attempt to maintain the authority of any vestiges of the other two mysteries (most notably in the form of the modern political State) as mere empty words. Once there has been a recognition that all these vestiges of spiritual authority in the modern world are illusory and that we human beings are using our intelligence purely to take care of the economic basis of our physical life, which is something the animals do without the benefit of intelligence,... we shall see the beginning of a great feeling of shame. And then the turnround will come. Then will come the realisation that a renewal of spirit and culture is needed.'[5]

Some forty years after Rudolf Steiner gave these lectures on cultural and social history in the first Goetheanum, Sir Charles (C.P.) Snow presented his famous Rede lecture on "The Two Cultures and the Scientific Revolution" at the Senate House in Cambridge,[6] a lecture which started a fierce debate lasting through the next decade or so. Snow's thesis had certain points in common with Rudolf Steiner's, with the crucial difference that Snow regarded scientific materialism as an ultimate end rather than as a death-process bearing within itself the seeds of cultural and social rebirth. Like Steiner, Snow perceived the vacuity of the grandiose attempt by especially English "literary intellectuals" to hold on to the vision of illusory wisdom and imperial grandeur which the British Empire came to express; and he regarded them as responsible – through their attitude of superiority and snobbery – for the cultural divide which he discerned between science and the humanities, between applied science and pure science, between doing and thinking, between the working-class and those from higher echelons of society.

What is being described in both these pictures is a world in which the old pagan wisdom, and the authority that went with it, no longer has any valid place. This is that spiritual wisdom that inspired the ancient post-Atlantean cultures of the East and enabled the Magi to find the Child and bring him their gifts. As we look back to C.P. Snow's analysis after a further forty years, we may conclude that the trends that he describes have reached a certain culmination. The capacity of modern technology to bring about changes in the way we live has far outrun the mind's ability to encompass them (still less to give them direction). The only star that is looked towards for guidance and inspiration in our time is money; and yet it is palpably obvious that those who have managed to acquire financial assets in large quantities – and have therefore become idols of success in our society – are far from being wise. Indeed, the modern money-market is more like a repository of anti-wisdom, fuelling a social divisiveness and egocentricity of atom bomb-like power. Not for nothing did John Davy, in his remarkable essay *Scientific Progress and the Threshold*,[7] associate the consciousness of the "Kings" in our time with, for example, the work of nuclear physicists. And whereas the modern "Kings" have descended from cosmic heights into the depths of an utterly earth-bound, atomistic conception of man and the world, the gesture of the "Shepherds" is to strive upwards from their earthly fastnesses to the world of cyberspace; for the immense unconscious hunger for reunion with the heavenly world which John Davy discerned in the 1960s in the technological achievements which made space-travel possible has now found expression in the Information Technology revolution. The motivating force behind modern technological developments is an overwhelming longing to transcend the sense of isolation engendered by the materalistic paradigm, a hunger for union – or fusion – with the whole. Whatever our karmic background, we as human beings of today share in one way or another in this terrible dichotomy between the cold darkness of the modern kingly consciousness and the blind, all-devouring hunger of the modern shepherd consciousness. A simple illustrative example could be drawn from the world of music: on the one hand there is the mathematical complexity and impenetrability of typical works of modern serious "classical" music, and on the other the increasing development of the shepherd-like folk tradition into melody-less rock, heavy metal and rap.

This analysis can be further illustrated by considering the whole theme of communication in our time. The late twentieth century would appear to be the age of communication *par excellence*. Never have there been so many ways of receiving and imparting the latest infomation, ranging from ever more bulky newspapers and numerous radio and television channels to the wealth of information that can be sent along telephone and other telecommunications networks; never has it been so easy to travel, with a range of options for getting from one place on the globe to the other with ever increasing speed; never has it been so possible to purchase items of merchandise from all over the world under one roof, as modern supermarkets vie with one another to represent the perfect global market-place.

It is, however, as well to be clear as to what these various networks are seeking to achieve and which aim or ideal they are serving. What is actually meant by the term "modern communications"?

It is instructive to consider the three categories delineated above from a `threefold' point of view (in the sense of the tasks of the three spheres of man's being as expressed by Rudolf Steiner in the Foundation Stone Meditation). The so-called information media serve largely to distract the individual's attention from the true task of the cultural sphere, namely, the practising of "spirit-vision", in other words, the quiet pondering over, or digesting, of one's experiences through the activity of thinking. The Government's determination to dominate education is a very clear example of the way in which this free space is being invaded in our time to an unprecedented degree. As for the ease with which we can now circumnavigate the globe in various kinds of vehicles, this represents an enormous hindrance to the practising of "spirit-awareness/ contemplation", an essential aspect of which is becoming truly aware of, and awake to, our fellow human beings. Many people in our time travel to far-flung destinations, and yet do not even know – or cannot get on with – their neighbours. Finally, the way that most of us have perforce to exchange wares with one another precludes the effective practising of "spirit-remembering"; for in a modern supermarket it is well-nigh impossible to know how and by whom the items that one purchases have been produced, still less to feel gratitude and wonder at the natural processes involved. By applying the "threefold" test even in this somewhat aphoristic, symptomatological way, therefore, one arrives at the impression that the communications systems of modern times are serving an aim which is diametrically opposed to the aims and intentions of the anthroposophical path and of the Michael age. Indeed, the first (spiritual-cultural) and third (economic) spheres have been inverted: the former is a hive of activity, of constant messages and oral and visual intrusions into the individual's private space, a domain of anti-freedom, whereas the latter is like a temple of worship (consider the very architecture, for example, of banks and supermarkets), a realm of anti-brotherhood; while the second directly hinders the working of Christ in the encircling round.

With this background in mind, it becomes possible to discern what modern commnications are intended to achieve. The conclusion suggested by the evidence of the above three categories is quite startling; for it would appear that the aim is to *prevent* the individual from communicating – respectively – with the spiritual world, with his fellow human beings and with the Earth (however strong the illusion that the contrary is the case may be). These communications systems are founded on the largely unconscious assumption that man is an atomistic individual entity who cannot – or who has no wish to – communicate with anything outside himself; and the whole intricate network of modern communications systems is designed to make this isolationism possible and yet also workable and – above all – bearable (by creating a gigantic illusion of togetherness). Most technological innovations of modern times are directed towards the aim of, on the one hand, bringing the world to the individual (or the proverbial mountain to Mohammed), who views it as a detached, non-participating (and, hence, non-responsible) observer, and, on the other hand, controlling – through State intervention – these atomised individual entities in such a way that some kind of social cohesion continues to be possible. This latter endeavour, in its turn, undermines the one quality – namely, man's capacity of thinking – which renders a different scenario possible. Meanwhile, the environmental side-effects of `bringing the world to the individual' are now – a generation after Rachel Carson published *Silent Spring* (1962) – viewed by many people as so catastrophically serious that they have opted out of the civilising drama which preceded and has ensued from the Incarnation of Christ.

*

A picture has been presented of a searing, and potentially disastrous, tension between the two principal streams of consciousness underlying Western civilisation – those of the "Kings" and the "Shepherds". What is urgently needed is for both streams to be working harmoniously together, thus creating a cultural wholeness not – as Snow tacitly advocates – by effectively abolishing one of its two main aspects but by enlivening dead thinking through the heart-warmth of imagination. To this common aim all anthroposophists of whatever karmic stream are – in theory at any rate – dedicated. This does not mean, of course, that the problems outlined above of non-collaboration between the two streams do not exist within the Anthroposophical Society. Indeed, van Manen expresses his view that the split within the Anthroposophical Society which came fully to manifestation in 1935 and did so much damage to the anthroposophical cause in this century came about because of an inability of the two streams to work together (and his suggestion that those individuals around

Marie Steiner who represented the "Platonic" aspect were not necessarily even Platonists merely adds further weight to this view). However, this should not be taken as implying that the situation is hopeless: one of the most remarkable features of the history of the Anthroposophical Society is that so damaging a split was able to be healed (at least in outward terms). How, then, might one characterise the present relationship between the Platonists and Aristotelians in the light of Rudolf Steiner's indication that the great teachers of Chartres are to return to an earthly incarnation at the end of the twentieth century?

The Anthroposophical Society since Rudolf Steiner's death has hitherto been outwardly remarkable more for the practical impulses that it has generated in the form of daughter movements (such as education, curative education, medicine, agriculture) based on indications given by Rudolf Steiner himself than for new spiritual-scientific research. Even the more "Platonic" element represented by many of the older generation around Rudolf Steiner was strongly focussed on the study of his books and lectures (especially the latter). The strongly "Aristotelian" character of the Anthroposophical Society as it has been bequeathed to the third generation of anthroposophists has been due as much to the cultural environment in which it has developed (for we live in a strongly "Shepherd"-dominated culture) as to the fact that, according to Rudolf Steiner, the great Platonic teachers of Chartres were only to appear at the end of the century. What is the place of the Platonists in this strongly Aristotelian world? One thing is transparently clear from the foregoing analysis concerning "Kings" and "Shepherds": it is no part of the modern Platonists' task – however great or wise they may be – to bring big ideas which everyone else is expected to follow, or in any way seek to rekindle the old (pagan) wisdom (of which the modern media, purveying endless information about everything, are a grim, inverted parody), still less point towards the teachings of someone less draconian in his rejection of old religious forms than Rudolf Steiner. The Christ whom they seek is to be found in the darkest depths of the isolated, alienated, individual human heart; and their task might be described as lighting little candles in this darkness, in all situations of daily life, so that each human soul, or anthropos, may find its own Sophia. This is, in a sense, a "horizontal" rather than a "vertical" task, one which has its focus in groups or communities of human beings endeavouring to work and live together on the Earth. Thus the Platonists' task is one which would lead them not to withdraw or separate from the forms and institutions established and built up mainly by the Aristotelians but to bring into them the leaven of their thinking capacity as a seed for cultural rebirth and social renewal. What has been built up over the years in the Anthroposophical Society since the Christmas Conference through the – essentially intellectual – study and implementation of anthroposophical ideas and indications is a substance of love, in which Christ can live and work. But until this substance of love is united in its Grail chalice with the formative forces of Imagination, one is not *conscious* of the presence of Christ, one does not *recognise* that this substance is the Substance of Christ. Bringing this light of recognition, or Imagination, is in the context concerned the particular task of the Platonists, thus enabling Michael himself to find the path from the Arthur stream (the last guardians of the Michaelic cosmic Intelligence), whose final earthly manifestation was the School of Chartres, to that of the Grail, where it can be engendered anew in the hearts and souls of human beings.[8]

What might this scenario look like in more practical terms? In the last of the lectures in the set published under the title *Ideas for a New Europe* (22nd February 1920), Rudolf Steiner expressed the view that, if all attempts to establish a threefold ordering of society on a wider front fail, it will be necessary to "work in tiny patches in the way we had to do in the case of the Waldorf School".[9] Yes, and work together with those who have, in the wake of Fritz Schumacher's adage, "Think globally, act locally", done so much to prepare the way for a more sustainable manner of life through their courage in opposing the excesses of industrial materialism.[10]

Images of little oases of renewal have cropped up with increasing frequency since Rudolf Steiner spoke these words. But it hardly ever happens that the same little oasis is envisaged as the location of *both* cultural rebirth and social renewal. In anthroposophical circles (Emerson College under Francis Edmunds would be an example) the cultural aspect tends to be emphasised, whereas in many areas of the "alternative society"or "Green" movement the emphasis is more on practical change or environmentalism. While I would not wish to make a definite pronouncement about the way in which this relationship between the anthroposophical movement and the "alternative society" movement may be understood karmically, I would submit that the establishing of oases of both cultural and social renewal would indeed be a meeting between the Seekers of Christ and the Servants of Michael, and ultimately between the Arthur stream and that of the Grail.

References

1 Published in English under the title *Twin Roads to the New Millennium* (Rudolf Steiner Press 1988.)

2 For a full analysis of these streams of consciousness, see Sergei O. Prokofieff's book *The Heavenly Sophia and the Being Anthroposophia* (Temple Lodge Publishing 1996.)

3 This is a different task from that of determining the karmic background of particular individuals, though of course a consideration of general trends should offer certain clues towards understanding these deeper realities.

4 Published together under the title *Ideas for a New Europe* (Rudolf Steiner Press 1992.) The former set was previously published in America in 1945 under the title *The Mysteries of Light, of Space and of the Earth.*

5 Ibid., lecture of 21st February 1920.

6 The lecture was given on 7th May 1959.

7 Originally published in *The Golden Blade,* 1964. Republished in *Hope, Evolution and Change* (Hawthorn Press 1985.)

8 These three sentences owe much of their content to Sergei Prokofieff's analysis of the challenge confronting the two streams at the end of the present century: see *Rudolf Steiner and the Founding of the New Mysteries*, second edition (Temple Lodge 1994), pp. 321-340 in particular. The interested reader is referred to this passage for a fuller picture.

9 See note 4.

10 The present article was, as a matter of fact, partly prompted by a most stimulating essay by Wendell Berry ('The Whole Horse') in *Resurgence* magazine (May/June 1998), contrasting (local) agrarian and (global) industrial economies, to the great advantage of the former.

Our Communion With The Dead

William Forward

The events of last August (the Omagh bombing) and the one before (death of Princess Diana) had the effect of focusing our minds on the crossing point from life into death and inevitably also on the question as to if and how we can continue to relate in a healthy way to those who have died. Do the bonds of karma that unite us in life extend across the threshold of death and if so, how? Could a re-membering of the dead into our daily lives shed some light on the nature of these relationships? The considerations that follow are intended to encourage exploration of these questions.

One of the most obvious and painful facts which we have to deal with when someone we love dies is that our customary channels of communication are broken off. Nevertheless the need to be in touch even if "only" in thought, remains. This is most strikingly felt in the now widespread custom of observing a minute's silence on occasions when the dead are commemorated. It can make possible an inner attentiveness and receptiveness which point in the direction of a new channel of communication. That this is also recognised by those who have died is indicated by W. Tudor Pole's account[1] of how he came to instigate the Big Ben Silent Minute in 1940 at the time of Dunkirk, of which he said, "There is no power on earth that can withstand the united co-operation on spiritual levels of men and women of goodwill everywhere."

The origin of the silent minute

The experience that promoted Tudor Pole occurred over twenty years earlier when he was with the British troops fighting the Turks outside Jerusalem. A young officer with him had a premonition which he expressed thus: "I shall not come through this struggle, like millions of other men in this war; it will be my destiny to go now. You will survive and live to see a more tragic conflict fought out in every continent and ocean and in the air. When that time comes, remember us. We shall long to play our part wherever we may be. Give us the opportunity to do so, for that war for us will be a righteous war. We shall not fight with material weapons then, but we can help you if you will let us. We shall be an unseen but mighty army. Give us the chance to pull our weight. You will still have "time" available as your servant. Lend us a moment of it each day and through your silence give us your opportunity. The power of silence is greater than you know...."

Such silence can of course also be practised by the individual and Rudolf Steiner indicated in 1916 how the moments before going to sleep and after waking are most propitious for focusing one's thoughts on the departed and for experiencing their responses in one's thoughts. In this way, then, one is consciously and deliberately making a space for the dead in the world that apparently succeeds them. It is also possible for the help of the living to be extended to those who have died. A remarkable example of such a relationship is documented in Doré Deverell's book "Light Beyond the Darkness".[2]

The dead can help us – Can we help them ?

Deverell describes her difficult relationship with her talented but tormented son who suffered from epilepsy. Years of allopathic treatment contained but did not help the condition, and he was never able to lead a fully independent life. She herself had to struggle with feelings of guilt, alcoholism, cancer and a difficult marriage. When he committed suicide in 1982, shortly before his thirty-sixth birthday, it seemed the inevitable had happened and that all prospect of helping him had now gone. Deverell's efforts to find a new direction led her to Rudolf Steiner College in Sacramento where she learned in conversation of Steiner's indication that the dead seek nourishment from the thoughts of the living and that by reading works with a spiritual content to the dead, having first strongly and warmly called them to mind, one can provide this nourishment. She then began with astonishing tenacity and devotion to do just this. After six months of daily readings she experienced her son saying in a dream as she was awakening, "I have finally found something that's helping me."

From the intimate dialogue between mother and son that gradually developed, Deverell came to feel that the tragic situation of a suicide – namely to remain in a kind of limbo until the pre-destined earthly life span has run its course – could be directly helped by her action in the daily reading. Just as by loving care one can further someone's progress on earth, it seems that the same can apply in relation to those beyond the veil of death. Indeed Steiner states in his lecture of 10th October, 1913 that the conscious understanding of the relationship in which we stand to the spiritual world, which it is the task of this epoch to begin to acquire, can only be so acquired on earth, but once having been achieved, it can be passed on to individuals on the other side and can be a helping influence on their destiny in the way described.

A working dialogue

Such a working together can take on dimensions that go well beyond the personal destiny of the individual. Indeed both Doré Deverell and her son worked out of the insights they had gained in this way to help other suicides and to dissuade other potential suicides. Still wider dimensions are evident in the remarkable account of the post-mortem correspondence between the German General Helmuth von Moltke and his widow Eliza as facilitated by Rudolf Steiner.[3]

Helmuth von Moltke was the nephew of the nineteenth century General of the same name and who enjoyed undying fame as the victor of the Franco-German war and was the co-founder of the German empire. The younger Helmuth von Moltke also became Chief of the General Staff, a position which he held at the outbreak of World War 1. A highly cultured and sensitive man as well as a respected General, he saw the outbreak of war as a tragic and undesirable inevitability, given the virtual abdication of responsibility by the Kaiser and the politicians to the military. The difficult task of adapting the Schlieffen Plan of war on two fronts to the conditions of the day was compounded by the Kaiser's whimsical over-estimation of his own military prowess, and his tendency to interfere. A mere month after the outbreak of war and the failure to achieve the strategically essential quick victory, von Moltke was relieved of executive responsibility. He died discredited and shaken on June 18th 1916.

As his relationship with the Kaiser grew strained, he began to develop closer ties with Rudolf Steiner whom he got to know through his wife Eliza. Over the two following years he was able not to change the course of outer events but to see them in a different light, both in the context of karmic relationships which Steiner was able to point out to him, and also of the true mission of the guiding spirit of the German people: a cultural impulse – not empire building.

At the same time Steiner's own work focused increasingly on an exploration of the destinies of whole peoples and of how they find their reflection in the destinies of individuals within them. The driving forces behind world history became a theme in his lectures.

When Helmuth von Moltke died suddenly on the 18th June 1916 Rudolf Steiner continued his contemplation of this individuality and out of the connection they had established was able to accompany him on his onward journey into the spiritual world. Over the next eight years he wrote down in the form of messages to Eliza von Moltke what he experienced as the thoughts of Helmuth. She in turn cultivated a relationship with her husband in meditation by reading him letters he had written her and by carrying him in her thoughts when she was reading or hearing spiritually inspired words.

They were able to follow how von Moltke saw his past life in retrospect and compared and contrasted it with his previous life's work in the 9th century. He later looked ahead to what would be his task in a future incarnation at the turn of the 21st century. "Now my will is united with the new weaving of the spirit that is beginning. Seeds must be planted in the ruins. The lie of our age has led us to ruin. The truth must lead to the building up of what is new."

At one level these communications are intimate and private, at another they illustrate the interrelation of a significant karmic group in terms of world history and at a time when a renewed conscious understanding of such relationships is beginning to develop. Now that they are published, they also provide insight into the destiny of Central Europe at a time when we clearly face a re-orientation of cultural, political and economic ties in Europe.

The Grail legend and those who have died

The Chretien de Troyes and Wolfram von Eschenbach stories date from the 12th – 13th centuries but they have a strong connection also with the life and times of the 9th century. It is fascinating to observe how the pre-occupation of the role of the European middle between East and West which characterised von Moltke's lives in the 9th and 20th centuries also has its echoes in the Grail legend, as does the question of the relationship between the living and the dead.

In Wolfram's epic we follow Parzival's biography from the meeting of his parents through to how his son Lohengrin takes up the kingship of the Grail castle after him. The quest for the Grail seems at the outset inevitably to lead him to the boundary between the living and the dead.

As he leaves home and unbeknown to him, his mother Herzeloyde dies of grief. He later encounters his cousin Sigune, cradling her dead lover Schionatulander. In this and her three subsequent meetings with Parzival she is together with her dead lover – an image of her role as mediator between the worlds of the living and the dead. After answering his naive questions about the incident she recognises him and calls him by his true name, explaining its meaning and drawing his attention to his heritage. His kingdoms of Norgals and Waleis had been usurped and her knight Schionatulander, had been defending them. The other cause for which Schionatulander had striven and which had cost him his life was to find the collar and leash of a setter which Sigune had asked him for. The background to this is elaborated in Wolfram's Titurel fragment and taken further in Albrecht von Scharfenberg's "Der Jüngere Titurel". The hound had sprung into Sigune's tent, trailing a beautifully stitched and decorated leash on which were written details of a twelve-fold path of virtue. The dog had dashed off before they could complete reading it and it had become Schionatulander's task to read it. In offering to help: "Cousin" Parzival said, "Your sufferings grieve me and my disgrace is great. If ever I have power to avenge it, I will settle the account" it can be seen that Parzival is taking up both causes which the dead man had to relinquish. Rudolf Meyer in his "Der Gral und Seine Hüter"[4] has shown convincingly how Parzival does indeed achieve each of the twelve virtues, culminating in that of "Minne" or selfless love, in the further course of his adventures.

Parzival's first visit to the Grail Castle, Munsalvaesche, comes about when he sets out to find his mother who, as we know (though he doesn't), is dead. He gets there in a dream-like state, his horse finding the way "for no man's hand was guiding it". His meeting with the Angler and his request for shelter take place at dusk, the meeting with the King Anfortas at night. He witnesses the magical process of nourishment by the Holy Grail. A picture perhaps of the mutual re-generation that takes place between human beings and the spiritual world at night.

On leaving in the morning, he has his second encounter with Sigune, still together with the dead Schionatulander, who is now embalmed. She explains to him the qualities of the sword he was given by Anfortas and chastises him for his failure to ask the question. Strikingly, she concludes, "You live, yet as far as Heaven's favour goes you are dead!" Once more, albeit in anger, Sigune has given Parzival guidance and enlightenment on his way.

Four years of fruitless searching for the Grail pass before Parzival once more comes close to the precincts of Munsalvaesche. He finds Sigune in a trackless forest living in an anchorite's cell beneath which Schionatalunder is now buried. More compassionate and conciliatory this time, Sigune explains that she now receives her nourishment from the Grail and directs him to follow the trail of Cundrie, the Grail messenger who had brought it that morning. Instead of Cundrie he meets a guardian of the Grail castle who challenges him with the words, "Munsalvaesche is unaccustomed to having anyone ride so near without fighting a desperate battle or offering such amends as those beyond our forest call 'Death'."

The outcome of the ensuing battle is that Parzival loses his horse in the ravine behind his opponent, but gains the latter's horse and thus continues his quest on a horse from Munsalvaesche. Something from the earthly world has to fall away in order that Parzival can cross over into the kingdom shared with the dead. When he later lets go the reins and allows the horse to guide him according to God's will, he is led to his uncle the hermit Trevrizent, who helps him to an understanding of the context of his quest.

When finally he does receive the grace of a return to Munsalvaesche it is after an experience of death. His sword shatters in combat with Feirefiz, his half brother, who says, "All your skill in combat cannot save you from death, unless I am pleased to spare you".

Guided this time by Cundrie, Parzival returns to the Grail Castle and there asks the healing question of Anfortas, "Uncle, what ails thee?" In doing so he opens in his heart a channel of communication with the dead. A final act of healing takes place when Parzival brings his wife through the forest to the castle and goes out of his way to seek out Sigune. She is found dead in an attitude of prayer over the tomb of Schionatulander in which she is then buried. Her role between the dead Schionatulander and the living Parzival is accomplished.

In a lecture given in Bern on the 9th November 1916 Rudolf Steiner describes in detail how much of what we tend to think of as our own inner guidance, whether in the form of imagination, inspiration or intuition, is in fact the working on into current earthly events of those who have died, who as they gain in objectivity and maturity in the time after death, influence the activity of those still on earth.

Specifically in relation to the Holy Grail and to how its guardians were perceived in former times he said in a lecture on the Holy Trinity on the 28th July 1922, "The dead remained with the living, and particularly outstanding revered personalities underwent a kind of noviciate in preparation for sanctity in the time immediately after their death, i.e. after their birth in the spiritual world....A number of these people, who were among the living while dead were, if they were among the select few, given the task of guarding the Holy Grail.... The Grail legend will never be completely understood if one does not know who its keepers really were. If one were to say for instance: then the guardians of the Holy Grail would not be real human beings – people at that time would have found it an absurd thing to say. They would have replied: do you shadowy figures who walk the earth believe that you are more than those who have died and who are now gathered round the Grail?"

This perspective can shed light on the enigmatic figure on Lohengrin, Parzival's successor as the Grail King. Known as the Swan Knight, he was called to the side of Queen Elsa of Brabant and could help her so long as he was not asked where he came from. In the above lecture Rudolf Steiner refers to the existence of an Order of the Swan "to which those people dedicated themselves who wished to enable the Grail Knights to work through them in the physical world. A human being through whom such a Grail Knight worked into the physical world was known as a swan.... One was not permitted to ask about the secret he bore within him."

One could imagine that the fruits of such work should be convincing enough in themselves, without people relying on the authority of a hero from the other world. Indeed the legend of

Lohengrin has it that once Elsa is manipulated into having to ask him about his origin, he leaves. The working of the company of the Grail thereafter remains shrouded in mystery.

We have thus seen that the quest for the Grail – a legend which has seen an unprecedented revival in the second half of this century – also involves becoming acquainted with, and eventually consciously crossing, the threshold between the living and the dead. The archetypal quality of the figures in the story also reflects this. It may be that those who are drawn to the legend sense the truth in it: that the ordering of our destiny in the future will increasingly involve the re-establishing of a true sense of community with the dead and an active working with them in such ways as are indicated by the examples of Tudor Pole, Deverell and von Moltke.

References

1 Tudor Pole, W. *The Silent Road,* Neville Spearman, 1960

2 Deverell, D. *Light Beyond the Darkness,* Temple Lodge, 1996

3 Meyer, Thomas (Editor) *Light for the New Millennium,* Rudolf Steiner Press, 1997

4 Meyer, Rudolf, *Der Gral und seine Hüter,* Verlag Urachhaus. Stuttgart 1958

Why on Earth are we here ?

Andrew Wolpert

Why did Christ have to come to earth? If God is omnipotent, could He not have redressed the imbalance in human evolution and brought about our salvation without the difficult and painful process of His Son's incarnation? Leaving aside the issue of divine omnipotence, the answer to these questions is inseparably connected to the reason why we ourselves are here on earth. What is possible here on earth that cannot be achieved in the spiritual world ? Why is it that matter matters?

There must be many levels on which one can gain an understanding of what Rudolf Steiner meant when he described the descent of the Cosmic Intelligence between the 5th and 9th centuries.[1] At one level it means that human beings acquired the individual and personal capacity to cognize how all phenomena are connected meaningfully. The corollary of that is that the sense impressions available to human beings are percepts that stimulate such conceiving of meaning. If that is true, then the perceptible world is a reliable expression of the spiritual world. The world of matter is waiting to disclose whatever we have reason to know of the world of spirit.

Human activity devoted to what the study of the material of the earth will reveal is a quest for the spirit, even if those thus actively engaged lack any consciousness of that. We interact with the earth constantly, we tread upon it, we move it, we take up what it yields as raw materials for our technology, we take it in with our senses, we ingest what it provides, and we encounter and interact with its substance in the plants, animals, and our fellow human beings. We are all engaged in the elaboration of the earth. Two particular instances of such engagement merit our attention in the context of this article. These endeavours are fired by an ideal to disclose what has been inscribed into the substance of the earth, in the one case by divine genius, and in the other by a human genius. Although these examples are historically and culturally very diverse and incomparable, they both illustrate the same point.

Paul Broadhurst and Hamish Miller, whose book *The Sun and the Serpent*[2] describes their discovery and mapping of certain earth-energy lines across Britain, are now preparing a second book based on their exploration of another earth-energy line across Europe. These ley lines are an aspect of how the earth embodies original cosmic forces that in earlier times were recognised and followed as indications for the timing and location of rites and the building of sacred monuments. Their re-discovery through these men's dedicated attention to what the earth still has to tell us has contributed significantly to our understanding of our own very different relationship to the same cosmic forces. Such evidence as their dowsing reveals illuminates something of the specific-place-bound relationship people had to the divine, and enhances our experience of the antithesis: the post-Golgotha whole-earth consciousness. It evokes awe for the spiritual and human beings who devoted themselves to the cultivation of such focused links between the cosmos and the earth, and inspires the most reverent gratitude for the part they have played in the whole evolutionary process. It is an ongoing process, one which has given us a relationship to the divine that challenges us now to sanctify whatever place it is that we happen to find ourselves in, by what we do, wherever we are. We are no longer obliged to go to sacred places, we can visit them today with different purposes, and freely, and gratefully acknowledge their meaning in our evolution. The significance of such acknowledgement for the spiritual beings still connected to ancient sacred sites should not be underestimated.

For eighteen years Dr Pinin Brambilla Barcilon has been engaged in the restoring of Leonardo's *Last Supper* in Milan. Her painstakingly exact work involves removing millimetre by millimetre not just the grime, but mainly the pigment that modern scientific techniques can reliably identify as not being original to Leonardo. In the artist's own life-time his masterpiece, painted on an unstable and damp north wall, began to flake, and it was subsequently touched-up and painted over many times. The first impression of its present state may be a shock to those who are familiar with the picture from reproductions that pre-date the current restoration: there is much less there than one expected, and it's all much paler. As you begin to take it in, in its totality and in its details, in its composition and in its colours, that first impression gives way to a very different experience. This scientist's dedication to an ideal through the physics, chemistry and optics of the material on the wall – the earth substance in which Leonardo inscribed his work – has resulted in a resurrection of Leonardo's deed. This assertion is bold and contentious, and cannot be substantiated just by descriptions of how alive, powerful, and urgent the picture now is. It is either experienced as such or not.

Broadhurst and Miller, and Brambilla Barcilon are examples of experts, very different in many ways but all fired by ideals in their taking up of tasks that involve the substance of the earth. Their work is characterised by patience, suspension of expectations, selfless dedication, perseverance, considerable adversity, and undaunted devotion. It is exemplary of the work that stands in such contrast to the sensationalism and fashion-driven pre-occupations of our cultural and political scene. Its courageous, single-minded fidelity to an ideal that nourishes the spiritual life identifies this work as uncompromisingly in the spirit of the times, in the service of the Spirit of our time. It is Michaelic. There are thousands and thousands of other, less well-known individuals whose engagement with the mineral realm is also of such vital spiritual significance. Some may be quite conscious of that, some may have inklings of it, others may for particular reasons be unaware of anything beyond what they are doing. Irrespective of the level of consciousness, such attention to the substance of the earth fired by an ideal nourishes the ideal itself, liberates it to wider recognition, and releases it for further metamorphosis. Our understanding of our earthly relationship to the divine can grow thanks to Broadhurst and Miller. Brambilla Barcilon has given Leonardo's inspiration new life.

And this work also changes the earth. The effect of such attention to the laws of the mineral world fired by the Logos prefigures in intensified measure what happens when we die. The ideals we live by inscribe their effects into the mineral substance that we call our bodies. When those bodies revert to the mineral realm of the earth, the substance of the planet is changed by the extent to which the ego forces have worked into the resisting flesh. The pigment Leonardo used was changed by the extent to which he brought it into the service of his inspiration, making visible the artistic activity. Our bodies are changed by the extent to which we bring them into the service of our destiny, making visible our activities, artistic or otherwise. The planet is changed by the destiny that it enables.

All this is to explore the symbiosis, the mutuality that lives between spirit and matter. Only through an understanding of the interdependence of Logos and earth, Ego and flesh, will the reflecting role of the mineral realm be seen. Not a passive mirroring in which the glass is indifferent to what it shows. But a spiritual deed by which matter sacrifices the display of its own nature to make visible something else. In the realms of the plants, the animals, and humanity the mineral substance manifests and makes visible the forms of these realms. Being visible in the world they can be known. In the case of a conscious ego, that self-knowledge is a reflected experience, made possible by the substance of the earth. It is on what can come about through such ego-consciousness that the future of human-earthly-cosmic evolution now depends, and the mineral realm, as the substance of the earth, provides the ground for that, literally, and also by giving us the bodies by means of which we can know ourselves.

All the processes of change that have been described here go through their metamorphic cycles irrespective of the consciousness of the beings involved. However, the process that leads to ego-consciousness has the particular potential that it can be identified with the incarnation of the Logos – with what the St John Gospel refers to as "The Word became flesh." If a human being grasps this Christ connection, then the same processes of change are not merely metamorphic, but evolutionary. That ingredient of Christ-consciousness is a leaven that transforms everything: it has the power to change the whole person, right down into the mineral substance of the flesh, and then the earth itself to which the discarded but transformed body returns. The process of the incarnation of the Logos into human flesh and then into the earth is re-enacted again and again, in small, humble, and as yet incomplete but inextinguishable human deeds for the future.

The recognition of Christ in the sense meant here is to know in oneself the life-affirming, renewing, enabling and empowering source of unlimited love that yearns to illumine and know every aspect of oneself and of every human being in the momentous business of our individual and shared destinies, the becoming of what we are not yet. It is also to know it in the other. It could be described as the uncompromising love for the truth. It is not just piously to believe the gospels, and it does not necessarily involve accepting either the gospel accounts of the life of Jesus, or even acknowledging the name Christ. This author enjoys a cultural destiny that invites him to make a causal connection between this mighty all-human experience and the being of Jesus Christ and the event of two thousand years ago in Palestine. The leavening efficacy of acknowledging this life-affirming source of love does not depend on what name it is given. It is necessary today to affirm this non-exclusive approach to the name of the Being who mediates that Love. However, pace the politically-correct inclusive-terminologists, that need for open-mindedness does not exclude identifying Him by the name Christ. It is beyond the scope of this article to explore why it should be the destiny of some people for a time in their biographies, to carry a conscious paradigm of the world that is ostensibly atheist and materialist, while at the same time living out of a burning, life-determining inner connection with this evolutionary principle. Its relevance to other religions and cultures is one of the most burning questions in a humanly all-inclusive, whole-earth consciousness, not just in terms of religions and faiths, but also in education, history, sociology, anthropology, and anything else that is ecumenical in the original meaning of this Greek word – belonging to the inhabited earth.

A meditant who lives with the words of St Paul, "not I, but Christ in me" pursues an individual path. The solitariness of such inner work derives its fulfilment from the unavoidable social and communal context of our human existence. Every man is an island connected to every other human being by the earth we all stand on, by the tide of time we all move in, by the air we all breathe, and by the sun that illumines us all. The process of individualisation is predicated on the inherited bonds of race, nation, tribe, and family. And this separation remains unfulfilled without the corresponding more or less freely chosen reconnections to partners, friends, colleagues, and other companions with similar cultural, political, or religious interests. The very aloneness of the turning points from the constellations we are born into to the configurations we weave around us as life goes on is an essential earth-experience. The separating, isolating, atomising consequences of material existence discharge their task nowhere more rightfully than in the barrenness of soul that leads to a sense of self and initiative. If the way out is then the cushion of self-reliance, and independence, it may be a gentle or a hard destiny that exposes the illusions of self-sufficiency and leads to social opportunities of inter-dependence and mutual support. Nowhere in the spiritual worlds could such crises be experienced in solitude. Only on the isolating earth do we experience ourselves apart from the others, and only in the context where matter alone appears to matter can our inseparable destiny companions for a time be unrecognised and unknown.

It is just in the separation that earth existence makes possible that the Logos can manifest as a sense-perceptible phenomenon that we are responsible for generating and recognising. Such is the potential of human dialogue. For this the Word became flesh. For this we can speak to each other and articulate our intuitions also to ourselves. Re-cognising is to know again what we once knew, it is not the same as remembering. Individually and freely I affirm as objective fact what once I was part of: I could not *know* it then without the distance that this earthly separation provides, and the recognising at once overcomes the separation. And it is in the recognising what has thus incarnated and died into words that we redeem the beings whose sacrifices support the existence of the reflecting mineral realm. In the recognising there is a resurrection. Conversation is the ground on which this dying and rebirth can happen.

Who do we have such momentous dialogues with ? Could I converse thus with anybody? Must not each such interlocutor necessarily be apart from me and also a part of my destiny?

We are part of many different constellations, configurations and circles of destiny. Some of these may not manifest as visible groups on earth, some may not be recognised, some may be dimly discerned, some may be very clearly seen, and then also cultivated consciously; and each of these groups may have a specific task. In the context of this article we can identify one such destiny group that does not have a purpose specific only to those who recognise their membership of it – it is a task recognisable by every human being as part of earth existence. It would be the subject of a further study to explore what the significance is of particular individuals awakening to that general human task and acknowledging it in their membership of this particular karmic group – the Anthroposophical Society.

Let us briefly recall some of the foregoing ideas with greater focus on our opening question. Rudolf Steiner described how Christ connected Himself to human evolution on earth three times ever more intensively during the Lemurian and Atlantean epochs.[3] At the Mystery of Golgotha Christ's commitment to human earthly evolution took another decisive step, and the subsequent descent of the Cosmic Intelligence provided yet further intensification of what human beings can achieve on earth. Just what that is, expressed most essentially, is the possibility of knowing the spiritual world. Our earth existence and its experience of matter separate us from the spirit. Only such separation can provide the objectivity on which knowledge depends. We leave the spiritual world to know it. Not to remember it. That is what we come to earth for and what the matter and processes of natural science have enabled us to learn. We think of the benefits of science in our technological achievements, but these are the fortunate or disastrous consequences of the epistemological training process nature provides. The most valuable consequence of science is that it has taught us to *know*, it has taught us the reliability of cognition. It is because of the connections Christ has made with us on earth that such a knowing is possible.

It is just this possibility of knowing the spiritual world that is affirmed by membership of the Anthroposophical Society. The only condition of membership is to consider valid the kind of research such as is done at the Goetheanum. It is not to subscribe to any of the content of spiritual – scientific research, but to the method of spiritual science. To join the Anthroposophical Society is to affirm in a karmically focused and intensified deed just what it is that we have joined in reincarnating onto the earth: a human community that can know its spiritual origins and destiny.

The life experiences that lead an individual to affirm this reality are themselves intimately bound up with the biographies of all the many other individuals we have karmic connections with. Such connections manifest in this life, manifested in previous lives, and also in our time together between incarnations when together we experienced spiritual companionship and together shaped our joint and individual pre-birth intentions. It is therefore absolutely organic that that shared affirmation of the possibility of knowing the spiritual world should strive to bring us into corresponding companionship on earth. The archetype of incarnation also stands behind and enables such spiritual companionship to manifest in the sense-perceptible dimension of the Anthroposophical Society.

Connecting oneself with such a group into the realm of matter with a signature in ink on a piece of paper (inscribing the sign of one's individuality into the earth) in the cause of spiritual science is a karmic commitment to that cause and to the group who have already affirmed it. And it is a karmic reality because behind that group stands the consciously destiny-uniting deed of one who took this step as an entirely new deed and as a risk. Rudolf Steiner's unreserved connection to the group who would affirm the earthly purpose of humanity in their membership of the Anthroposophical Society was possible because behind that stands the deed of One Who took precisely the same kind of destiny-uniting step as an entirely new deed and as the seal of a process that affirms the meaning and purpose of human evolution on earth.

References

1 Lecture (Torquay, 21. 8. 24) GA 240 published in *Karmic Relationships Vol. VIII*, Rudolf Steiner Press, London, 1975.

2 Pendragon Press, 1991.

3 This is described in two lectures included in GA 152 published separately in English as *Pre-Earthly Deeds of Christ,* (Pforzheim, 7. 3. 14) Steiner Book Centre, Inc. N. Vancouver, 1976; and *The Four Sacrifices of Christ* (Basel 1. 6. 14) Anthroposophic Press, 1981.

The Karmic Community of Samuel Hartlib, John Dury and Johann Amos Comenius.

Ken Gibson

The name of Johann Amos Comenius is well known in anthroposophical circles,not least because Rudolf Steiner spoke extensively about his occult background and his karmic connection to Francis Bacon.[1] Less known, however, are two other individuals, Samuel Hartlib and John Dury, who worked together with him on a range of educational, social and religious projects. All of these projects were inspired by the Pansophy of Comenius, which then became the basis of their efforts to reform education, to promote ecclesiastical peace, and to implement social reform. The trio remained in close contact all their lives in pursuit of their ideals and, at the same time, built up a network of European contacts. Although it is not possible in this short article to discuss in any detail all of these activities, it is hoped that the general background and brief description of their work that follows will stimulate interest and provoke further research.[2]

Europe, in the early seventeenth century, was full of conflict. The counter-reforming efforts of the Roman Catholic powers sought to limit the sphere of Protestant influence, and this contributed greatly to the growing political and religious strife. This was fuelled by national and dynastic rivalries, political intrigue and power struggles within the existing two hundred European states. The fierce conflict of the Thirty Years

War set Europe alight, bringing devastation, ruin and distress into the lives of many people. Over in England, from about 1630 onwards, there was also growing political and religious tension because of the misguided policies of King Charles who was less tolerant to the Puritan faction within the English Church than his father, James I. This, coupled with Charles's enforcement of extra-parliamentary taxation, his questionable religious policies and his refusal to call a Parliament for eleven years, led eventually to a complete breakdown of his government and the outbreak in 1642 of the English Civil War. Within this melting pot of religious dissension and political strife the small karmic community of Hartlib, Dury and Comenius began their life-long endeavour to unite the fragmented cultural life of Europe.

To identify Samuel Hartlib, John Dury and Johann Amos Comenius as a karmic community is perhaps imposing a concept upon them of which they were not consciously aware. Looking at them, however, with an interest in destiny configurations, it is possible to discern how a strong karmic impulse brought them together. This was recognised by John Dury in a letter to Sir Cheney Culpepper when he said "though our taskes be different, yet we are all three in a knot sharers of one anothers labours and can hardly be without one anothers helpe and assistance". This strong spiritual bond later manifested itself in physical form by the signing of a pact or sacred covenant by the three of them in 1642, where they pledged themselves to promote religious peace, to educate Christian youth and to reform the study of true wisdom. Nothing, they agreed, would be done without seeking each others' advice and agreement. Of especial importance in the pledge was the offer of continued assistance to each other in all practical and spiritual matters. It is possible to suggest that this spiritual bond drew them to the area around Elbing in West

Prussia where they first met and which was to have a formative influence on them for the remainder of their lives. Hartlib was born here, and in nearby Polish Lesno the exiled Czech community, to which Comenius belonged, had its centre. Elbing was also the place where Dury worked as a minister to a company of Merchant Adventurers. Significantly this area was famous for its tradition of religious toleration, and because of this many German and Dutch refugees fleeing from the Thirty Years War began to settle here. The Mennonite farming communities began to become established and the Moravian Anabaptists experimented with their own democratic style of community living. Even more significant for this area was the widespread circulation of the writings of Jacob Boehme and Valentin Weigel and the growing awareness of Rosicrucianism. A few years later, however, the area was invaded by the Hapsburg forces and the impulse which was trying to find expression was effectively stifled.[3]

In 1626 Samuel Hartlib, seeking refuge from war torn Europe, made a short visit to England. He returned briefly to Elbing, but finally settled in London in 1628 and remained there until his death in 1662. John Milton dedicated his tract *On Education* to Hartlib and said of him: "he was a person sent hither by some good providence from a farre country to be the occasion and the incitement of great good to this Island". Throughout his life Hartlib exercised influence in a wide variety of areas. He was involved in, among other things, education, chemistry, horticulture, technological development and military engineering. He collected and disseminated information on books, manuscripts, new inventions and scientific discoveries which led him to become known as *The Great Intelligencer of Europe.* Hartlib and Dury were also very much concerned with the welfare of the less fortunate members of London's population and became actively involved in numerous projects to relieve the poor. During his residency here Hartlib was in touch with the leading political figures of the day and he formed a warm friendship with the Parliamentary leader John Pym. Both were interested in employing the services of the Bohemian inventor Johann de Berg whose assistance they wanted in a mine draining enterprise in Northamptonshire. Hartlib remained intensely interested in the Pansophy of Comenius and was responsible for the publication and distribution of two of his writings in England. For Hartlib the pansophic ideas of Comenius infused with the inductive methods of Francis Bacon would provide the unifying principles needed for his diverse and wide-ranging practical projects. He thought that the early 1640s marked the beginning of a new age when the three of them could begin building a new society. This found expression in a work published in 1641 with the title of England's Thankfulnesse:

"Yet now behold we live, and instead of desolation, the breaches of old are repaired, instead of confusion, the foundations are laid for many generations to build upon, and instead of feare, a great door is opened to us, that we shall be firmly and fully settled in all abundance of peace and truth.[4]

John Dury shared Hartlib's vision of a new and unified cultural life but his tasks were different. He was by birth a Scotsman, but because his father had been banished abroad in 1606, he received his education in Leiden, later attending the university to study Theology. In 1624 he was called to be the minister to a group of English and Scottish Merchant Adventurers in Elbing where he formed his friendship with Hartlib in 1627. Under the influence of the Swedish Privy Councillor Godemann Dury, in 1628, was persuaded to devote his life to the task of Christian Union and achieving the peaceful settlement of the confessional conflicts within the European Churches. It is also known that during this time Dury formed friendships with Johann Valentine Andreae and others interested in forming Christian societies. From about 1628 onwards Dury began to travel extensively in Europe with the intention of persuading the most prominent figures within the Church to find ways to heal their differences. Dury was away on one of these trips when he, together with Comenius, received a call to come to England. This call was heard by all the members of Parliament when John Gauden diverged from the main content of a sermon he was giving before the House of Commons to announce:

"Here give me leave by way of short digression, in so great and publique an Assembly, to recommend to your favour, the noble endeavours of two great and publique spirits, who have laboured much for truth and peace, I mean Comenius and Duraeus; both famous for their learning, piety and integrity, and not unknowne, I am sure, by the fame of their works, to many of this honourable, pious and learned Assembly".[5]

The initial intentions of the trio in England were to found a college where the ideals of pansophic learning could be promoted. With Comenius as its head, a small group of scholars would assimilate the most advanced knowledge to develop a unified understanding of the material and spiritual worlds. From the three existing colleges of Savoy, Winchester and Chelsea the choice fell on Chelsea College – founded in 1607 – but their plans never came to fruition because of the impending conflict in England and the outbreak of the Irish Rebellion. The long-term intentions of Hartlib and his group do, however, find their reflection in a small tract presented to Parliament just after the arrival of Dury and Comenius in England. This utopian tract contained a wide-ranging vision of economic and social reforms. It was written by another of Hartlib's circle Gabriel Plattes, who gave it the name of Macaria (Islands of the Blessed). This tract is similar in structure and presentation to the genre of Utopian writings that appeared during the sixteenth and seventeenth centuries throughout the whole of Europe. Its main inspiration, however, is probably from the utopias of Sir Thomas More and Caspar Stiblinus. Macaria takes the form of a dialogue between a Scholar and Traveller who first meet in the Royal Exchange in London and later take a walk on Moorfields. The Traveller describes his visit to a "Kingdom called Macaria [where] the King and Govenours doe live in great honours and riches, and the people doe live in great plenty, prosperitie, health, peace and happiness, and have not halfe as much trouble as they have in these European Countrys". During the course of this dialogue the Traveller describes a society which contains the political and social forms which would solve the problems facing the English state at this time. The government of Macaria retains the Monarchy but the sovereign is to a certain extent controlled by a Great Council who are, unlike the previous eleven years, allowed to meet annually. To control the economy there are six committees concerned with Husbandry, Trade, Fishing, Trade by Land, Trade by Sea and New Plantations. It is the responsibility of each of these committees to develop each of their activities to the fullest extent in the interests of the Commonwealth. In the religious and spiritual realms a set of "Infallible Tenets" are given to the ministers with the intention of eliminating religious dispute and bringing about the longed-for religious peace. From a modern perspective the legislation of Macaria seems somewhat draconian. For example, landowners who persistently neglect the cultivation of their land lose their entitlement to it. Moreover, a minister of religion who publishes new opinions to the "Common people...shall be accounted a disturber of the publick peace, and shall suffer death for it". To regulate wealth all inherited property is taxed at one-twentieth of its value and the revenue used for agricultural improvement and the building of roads and bridges. Another important element in Macaria is the formation of a "College of Experience" along the lines of Bacon's Solomon's House. This institution places great emphasis on the role of science to improve medicine, agriculture and technology. The scientists or natural philosophers are placed in the service of the Commonwealth with a pledge to develop inventions and remedies for the overall improvement of the health and welfare of the citizens of the state. The most innovative aspect is the suggestion that ministers of religion should be trained as Physicians because, as the Traveller suggests, "of the diversitie of natures, complexions, and constitutions, which they are to know, for the cure of soules, as well as bodies".[6]

Except for this final point it might be assumed that the writer of Macaria places too great an emphasis on the practical improvement of society. With his idealised vision of a stabilised economy containing full employment, the creation of wealth for all citizens of the state and full regulation of trade Macaria seems, at one extreme, very utilitarian. To balance this picture out it is worth taking into consideration the words of Rudolf Steiner who when speaking about the Rosicrucian Brotherhoods says that "Comenius was a man who came into contact with numerous secret fraternities in the course of his life...[he] entered into a real relationship with them, trying to influence them. How he was able to influence them is particularly shown in what he says in his Pansophia". Given Hartlib and Dury's karmic connection with Comenius it can be assumed that they also were inspired by the impulse of Rosicrucianism as were many of their circle in England. Indeed there is sufficient evidence of this from Hartlib's early contacts in Europe and the ensuing correspondence.[7]

Before coming to England Hartlib was in contact with a group of like-minded individuals who wished to set up a utopian community somewhere in Europe. This group or society formed one of the many semi-secret brotherhoods, mentioned by Rudolf Steiner, that sprang up in Central Europe at this time. This society took the name of Antilia and probably came into existence just before the outbreak of the Thirty Years War. The correspondence that passed between Hartlib and other members is rather fragmentary, but significantly the name of the Swedish Privy Councillor Godemann appears who, it seems, "is in agreement with this great work". This provides a further link to John Dury who, during his extensive European travels, could have visited the brotherhoods and passed on information to Hartlib and Comenius. Moreover, Hartlib had ongoing contact throughout his life with the scientific community of Joachim Jungius through whose genius, as Ernst Lehrs informs us, "the true Rosicrucian impulse was brought to expression".[8] A further contact who had Rosicrucian connections is that of Louis De Geer who was instrumental in bringing Comenius to Sweden after his visit to England and who also financed the activities of both Dury and Comenius. Furthermore, Hartlib corresponded with Johannes Rulice, an exiled minister from the Palatinate who was also a member of De Geer's society in Amsterdam. More compelling evidence for Comenius's membership of a Rosicrucian brotherhood is provided by his friendship with Philip Van Zesen. Van Zesen founded a society in Hamburg in 1643 with the name of the Rose Brotherhood and at a later date a brotherhood of the same name was established in Amsterdam. The password of both these organisations was Pax and they therefore became known as the Order of Peace. Membership was restricted and later in 1669 when it was considered that enough members had been admitted another society was established with the name of the Lily Brotherhood. When admittance to this was full a third society was founded with the name of the Carnation

Brotherhood. The Rose Brotherhood was divided into nine sections each with nine brothers. The Lily Brotherhood into seven sections each with seven brothers and the Carnation into five sections with five brothers.

Whether Hartlib or Dury formally entered into any of the brotherhoods remains unknown, but what these contacts provide is an indication of a positive impulse entering into England from the broader karmic community of the Rosicrucians through the much smaller karmic community of Hartlib, Dury and Comenius.[9] Moreover, the fact that this karmic group came together in Europe at a historically significant point to fulfil a specific mission is indicative of the karmic forces at work in the destinies of individuals, groups and nations.

References

[1] Rudolf Steiner spoke of this in many lectures but more especially in the series of lectures entitled *Karmic Relationships* given in various European cities in 1924. I would like to thank Frank Mulder for providing me with a print-out of his yet unfinished data-base on all the references where Rudolf Steiner spoke about Comenius. Frank also provided me with some of the information on Louis De Geer.

[2] To keep footnotes to a minimum I have only referenced those works on which I have substantially relied. Biographical information on Hartlib, Dury and Comenius is taken from: Charles Webster, *The Great Instauration: Science, Medicine and Reform, 1626-1660* (London 1975). Daniel Murphy, *Comenius: A Critical Assessment of his Life and Work* (Irish Academic Press, Dublin, 1995); J. Minton Batten, *John Dury: Advocate of Christian Union* (Chicago 1944) Mark Greengrass, *Hartlib and International Calvinism,* Proceedings of the Huguenot Society of Great Britain Volume 25 1993 pp. 464-475. G.H. Turnbull, *Hartlib, Dury and Comenius: Gleanings from Hartlib's Papers* (Liverpool 1947). The papers of Samuel Hartlib are now available on CD ROM and contain a vast amount of information on these three individuals. Additionally some of Comenius's Latin correspondence from the papers are presently being translated to be published in the near future.

[3] Most of the information for this paragraph is supplied by: Charles Webster, *Macaria, Samuel Hartlib and the Great Reformation,* Acta Comeniana (Prague) Volume 2 1970 pp. 147- 164.

[4] A complete copy of this tract is printed in Charles Webster, *Samuel Hartlib and the Advancement of Learning* (Cambridge University Press 1970) pp. 90-97. This excellent book contains a good introduction to the educational ideas and activities of all three individuals.

[5] Sermons before Parliament became a regular occasion from 1640 onwards

[6] For a modern reprint of this tract see : Charles Webster, *Samuel Hartlib and the Advancement of Learning* (Cambridge University Press 1970).

[7] Some of this correspondence is found in G. H. Turnbull, *Hartlib, Dury and Comenius.*

[8] Dr. Ernst Lehrs, *The Rosicrucian Foundations of the Age of Natural Science,* Supplement to Anthroposophical Movement Volume XI No. 23 1934. I would like to thank Margaret Jonas for supplying me with a copy of this article.

[9] The information on the Brotherhoods is taken from a number of secondary sources including: Ludwig Keller, *Die Bruderschaften zum Heiligen Kreuz und andere Akademien, Logen und Kammern des 17. Jahrhunderts.* Monatsheft der Comenius-Gesellschaft Band 3 January 1911; Karl. F. Otto jnr, *Zu Zesens Zunften* in: Ferdinand Van Ingen, *Philipp van Zesen 1619-1669 Beiträge zu seinem Leben und Werke* (Franz Steiner, Wiesbaden 1972). It is worthwhile bringing to attention the work of Ludwig Keller who in the latter part of the last century and the early part of this century did some excellent work on the Brotherhoods of the seventeenth and eighteenth centuries. What marks Keller out from his contemporaries is that he takes a very positive attitude in his studies towards their impulse. This is more than can be said for some present-day historians who are more than sceptical about their very existence.

Japan and my destiny

Fumiko Chikami

My Parents

My father was born in 1921 in Toyotsu, a small village in Kyushu Island in the south of Japan. Toyotsu, which means a rich place by the water, is situated in the peaceful countryside between two rivers. To the south, the gentle hills lead to the Holy Mountains where hermits went for spiritual training, and to the west is the coal mining district beyond which lay the old capital of Kyushu island. The sea with its swift currents is close by to the east, and about 50 km north are the straits of Korea. The distance between Korea and Kyushu island is not great, but rough seas separate the two countries and guarded Japan from several attempted invasions in the long past.

My grandfather came from the warrior class and ran a small stationery business in the village. My father's mother died when he was a small child and he grew up without a warm family. However, he was a strong, persevering and clever boy. In 1940 at the age of 19, he graduated from the military college and was sent to China as an officer. During an exercise my father was nearly killed by a misdirected bullet, which went through his throat. He fell from the horse but his riding boot got stuck in the stirrup, and he was dragged along for several hundred meters. Since then his voice was very husky and low. I do not know exactly when he was posted to Taiwan. He heard the news of the end of the war in the countryside of Taichun.

In the same year, my father met my mother. They went to live in Taiwan, which was under Japanese rule, before World War I. My mother's father was a policeman, her mother an active, inventive woman who was the centre of a large cheerful family. My mother, who was a gentle and studious girl, continued her studies at a college in Taipei and was teaching at a Japanese school in Taichun when she met my father. They were married and came back to Japan together with my mother's family. For the next seven years they lived in Toyotsu and had three daughters whom they named the child of truth, beauty and holiness.

Nature Child

During the early days of their life in Toyotsu, my parents got by day by day just as everyone did after the war. By the time I was born in 1949, my father had a job in a distant town and was commuting on a local train. One of my earliest memories with some sequence is about this period. According to my mother, I used to wander around the village alone or with friends. On that hot summer afternoon, I had the idea of going to the station to meet my father when he came back from work. The station was some way out of the village but I knew the way well. So I set out with a boy from next door. We left the village, went through the shady bamboo forest. We continued our way down the gentle hill and were on the white dust road leading to the station in the middle of rice fields. Then a small stream running along and below the road caught our attention. We were very hot and the water was so tempting. We left the road and went into the shallow water. As we walked in the clean knee-deep water, fish swam around our legs, which delighted us. The station and my father disappeared, and the thought of time did not exist yet – we were not quite four years old. All of a sudden, we found ourselves in the evening light and I sensed that I missed my father. We headed for home. It was pitch dark by the time we came to the bamboo forest. We walked in the dark in silence and saw a strange light approaching. I heard the rest of the story the next day and many times later. An old man living near the bamboo forest had found two small children and had carried me home while holding the boy's hand. My young parents had been worried and searched everywhere and were relieved to meet the old man on whose back I was fast asleep. Apart from this episode and some isolated moments here and there, I remember very little of the life in that quiet village. But there my soul and body were nourished not only by my family but also by the beauty and wonder of nature which supported me long afterwards.

Death and Awakening to Life

When my older sister was six, I four, and my younger sister only several months, my family moved from Toyotsu to the company flat in the small town where my father's growing steel company was situated. The day we left Toyotsu is clear in my hazy memory of early childhood. In the warm air of late spring, I said good-bye to my grandfather's flower garden, which I admired, and went to the small truck on which our furniture was loaded. I was, however, disappointed when I was lifted onto the passenger seat between the driver and my mother who was holding my younger sister: father laughing in the breeze at the back among the furniture. This move brought a complete change to my life for I was not able to wander in nature any more. I also started going to kindergarten. My kindergarten was run by a temple and situated in the temple grounds. We children gathered and played in the big hall where a large statue of Buddha sat and looked down at us.

In this town, a little over a year later, my father was killed in a train accident during work. He was thirty-three. My awareness of life started abruptly on that night when we were woken and taken to the company's hospital by my father's colleagues. There I saw my father lying on the bed no longer alive. Death had entered into my soul and I started looking at Life in contrast to Death. Yet I was not frightened by the image of Death. The young soul turned the question of "What is Death?" into "What is Life?" I started living that question from that night.

School Days

After the sudden death of my father, my life took another turn, for my mother went back to teaching, which at that time in Japan was the only profession which treated women and men equally. My mother was liked by her pupils and respected by the parents. I was proud of her and missed her when she was not able to attend kindergarten (and later school) events. As I started school, I quickly changed into an active, independent child full of imagination and her own world. The question of Life and Death was at the bottom of my perception and judgement. I became a sensitive observer of human life. My soul was consoled and filled with dreams whenever I visited my relatives in Toyotsu, with whom I spent many happy holidays.

In the Toyotsu countryside I was able to breathe freely. My mother also took us to her family's homes in and around Tokyo. At my grandparents' home near the sea outside Tokyo, the children of my mother's sisters and brothers gathered during the summer holidays and we had many adventures together. As nature was my friend and teacher, there I learnt important lessons from the sea, which inspired my imagination with awe and longing. As the holidays drew near, I looked forward to the long train journey between my home and Tokyo. It gave me new pictures of different places and the different lives of others. This awareness of a wider world was not common among my school friends in the provincial town. I was keenly aware of this difference too. Long before my teens, I became critical of teachers and their educational approach. By the time I went to high school, I was certain that it lacked guiding ethics and principles. Indeed, it was the time when the whole country was in the process of transformation, replacing the traditional Japanese ethics and way of life with the newly introduced Western values and criteria. I cannot imagine the confusion the grown-ups were living with in those post-war years. We children were left alone. In a way my generation grew up in a vacuum, while our parents were working hard rebuilding the country.

Buddhism

It was perhaps the uneasiness of the void that made some people turn to the new movement of Buddhism, which emerged at that time. My grandmother found the new Buddhist movement and urged all her children and grandchildren to join this religious group. My mother who was in mourning following my father's death joined the group readily. I grew up watching my mother pray in front of a large altar at home for a long time each evening. Gradually, I came to understand that she found peace and support in Buddhist teaching as well as in the religious community. We children did not join her prayers very often, which saddened her. However, I enjoyed accompanying her in her annual trips to the temple at the foot of Mt. Fuji. I sat with a large congregation of monks and visitors and prayed with them. I felt at home with the meditative and festive quality of the temple and monks' way of life, though Buddhist teaching remained abstract for me.

Later in my student days, I often visited ancient temples in Kyoto and Nara, the old capital of Japan. There I absorbed traditional Japanese ethics and values eagerly and felt immense pleasure and deep peace in the landscape of the temples. Walking in the shady moss garden of one temple or in the colourful maple garden of another, I observed that beauty of nature was harmonised with religious ethics to perfection.

Taiwan. Micronesia

I left home at the age of eighteen to study cultural anthropology at a university in Tokyo. I was very fortunate to have the opportunity to visit Taiwan and Micronesia during my student days. I felt close to Taiwan because of my parents' connection to that country, and gladly took the post of teaching Japanese in the ancient city of Taiwan one summer. Against all my expectations I experienced there a country preparing for war against the Chinese People's republic and communism. The total lack of freedom and the prospect of a future bound to war and hatred troubled and confused my mind. The reality of life in Taiwan was so different from that of Japan that the two countries seemed to be separated by distance and time, not at all like neighbouring countries living in the same age. Yet, when I thought about my own country, I realised that our world was intrinsically interrelated. The peace and freedom I enjoyed in Japan was not permanent; in fact, I found it very fragile. After two months in Taiwan, I left, feeling sadness and love for that country.

I went to Micronesia, US controlled territory after the war, as an assistant to a TV documentary programme team. The tropical beauty of the islands in the middle of the Pacific Ocean was a dream, and my heart rejoiced. Yet the reality I encountered there was painful and I was made sadly aware of the vice of our society. Western materialism had intruded into the life of the islands with alcohol and other imported goods for which men of the islands had become labourers. It was rapidly destroying the traditional values and the harmonious living in nature with the illusion of progress. Both in Taiwan and Micronesia, I met young people who were aware of the situation and were searching earnestly for ways of change. I felt sympathy for them and wished we knew the way to solve the riddle and conflict of our age.

Death of N. The plateau of Central Japan

It was the time of the world-wide student movement and of the end of Vietnam War. I heard the news of the US withdrawal from Vietnam from my Japanese American friend in Kyoto. The air of the international travellers' lodge lifted, and we celebrated the occasion joyously. However I was not able to follow the students' political activities. Though I was a questioning young woman with passion and idealism, I was aware that neither the students groups nor I possessed the vision or tools for change. I retreated into the nature of the vast plateau of Central Japan, which I found at the beginning of university life.

I found the space I needed to grow on an experimental farm established after the war by an American professor of my university (with financial support from the church in the US). There was a lodge at the farm where students came to work to experience the community life and agriculture. The nature of the plateau was very different from that of Toyotsu, but its pure vast beauty and deep tranquillity drew me back there holiday after holiday.

It was there my soul retreated after receiving the news of the death of my friend N, a young architect. The tragic death of a heroic figure at the beginning of his life, full of promise and dreams. It was at an early stage of our friendship, but I felt a strong affinity with this sincere and creative man. One night, his 19-year-old brother stabbed him in a moment of mental imbalance. I heard the message of death again, and suppressed it, but not for long. In the stillness of the nature of the plateau, one year later I finally faced my wounds and listened to the truth deep within. Beneath the wound left by the death of N. was another wound left by the death of my father a long time ago, yet still so fresh. Two deaths were urging me to take the unknown path of my own to find my own life's expression. I decided to leave Japan, for I could not find a vision of life in Japanese society.

Paul and The Journey to the East

I chose to come to England where I knew no one, with the immediate aim of studying the English language, but also to pursue the question born in me a long time ago: "What is life?" How do I live this transitory life on Earth? I wished to live a full, meaningful life and for that I needed a vision. In the summer of 1973, I left Japan and arrived in London at a city barrister's home on my 24th birthday. I lived and studied in London for the next three years. I enjoyed the studies, but it was not an easy time for I was isolated and could not see clearly where I was going. Still, I trusted my guiding star – my sense of destiny – which had brought me thus far.

Three years later my destiny took me to the south of France. There I met Paul, an expatriate, a linguist, a lonely traveller and my future husband. We recognised a kindred spirit in each other and were able to share the sense of a quest.

Through him and his friends back home and in France, I came to know the despair and the wishes of youth in Western society. I saw that their pain was the pain of our time, for across the cultures, all our souls have the stamp of our time. We worked and travelled throughout Europe for the next few years, and when we failed to settle down in the countryside in the south of France, we decided to leave Europe. We joined the dreams of the seeking souls of the West, the pilgrimage to the lands of mysteries and ancient teachings, the East. We passed through frozen Italy and Yugoslavia and entered the warmth of Greece where we hitched on land and sea. We walked through the desert of Egypt in the full moon, and conversed with ancient statues in temples half buried in sand. We reflected on our life by the Nile. Our souls traversed the Indian subcontinent, which blessed us with pictures of glory – coupled with the sight of misery – and we trekked the heights of the Himalayas with heavy hearts, loaded with questions. When we walked through the rustic countryside of Northern Thailand, I felt Asia and the end of our journey.

Japan and Life in Nature

After fourteen months' journey, we arrived in Japan. When I took Paul to Toyotsu, which my soul sought, I was deeply moved to be back in the nature of my birthplace. During the seven years of my absence, Japan had been transformed into the economic giant which our parents had striven for in the ruins of the war. We did not intend to stay there long. However, while working in Tokyo, our thoughts turned to family life in nature and we found a ruin in a small mountain hamlet in the middle of Kyushu. When our first daughter was one year old, we moved to the mountains in order to live in and learn from the wisdom of nature. Paul, never happy in his own country, felt he had arrived home there. For the next seven years, we were builders, farmers, carpenters, foresters, and I became the mother of two more children. Gradually an idyllic organic farm emerged out of our hard work, overcoming countless difficulties on the way. But we were not to be left in peace there long.

In our travelling we encountered time and again the signs of destruction and the sights of suffering our civilised living had brought to the world. Now through the farming life in the deep mountains of Kyushu, the painful cry of mother Earth reached my consciousness. I started seeing unbearable pictures of the destruction of nature and our living environment in Japan and abroad. The shock of Chernobyl was in its frightful beginning. The cry of despair from the tropical rain-forest of Malaysia and Brazil reached us, and we were moved to action. The distorted agricultural practice all over the world and in our village darkened our souls, and we witnessed with bitterness the massive transport of industrial and domestic waste into the beautiful mountains nearby.

Shadow and Light

It seemed as if there was nothing which was not born out of the destruction and exploitation of nature and people living close to nature. I vividly remember a dream I had at that time: I was standing in our field with the children. Suddenly the whole sky turned reddish-gold and I was falling to the ground. In silence, falling, I felt it was the end of all life. It was the most painful dream I have ever had. Our growing children brought the question of education home too. With my own emptiness in school days, I was keenly aware of the need for a different, holistic approach in education. It was then that a visitor from the city left me an extract of a book by Rudolf Steiner. His words left in me the deep impression of truth, and my heart was glad, for I recognised in the short passage the knowledge and vision I was yearning for. A small light was lit in the inmost recesses of my heart. By the time our third child was one year old, we had formed an international group with friends. Its aim was awareness of our living environment, and it attracted a large number of people in the district. We organised many campaigns, workshops and lectures, asking for change in our society. It was an extremely busy and fulfilling time, though we were never free from the awareness that the social and political issues we were addressing were gathering dark forces. I needed knowledge and clear vision, lack of which I keenly felt and suffered from. Our marriage was also under pressure. Though our aim of life was close, our starting-points, our cultural and individual backgrounds were very different. We were not able to overcome the different gestures and perceptions in our souls and our cultures.

England

When my youngest daughter was four, our marriage came to an end, and I left the mountains to tread the path for vision all over again. Having lived seven years in the beauty and tranquility of the mountains it was not easy to find the next footing. I needed to endure the sense of isolation and uncertainty for two years before my destiny called me back to England once more. I found a position as a supervisor in a Japanese boarding school in the Midlands. A new life in the large community of Japanese teenagers and British and Japanese staff began. I found a Steiner school for my two younger children, while my oldest daughter preferred the life on the farm with her father.

My work was to support and guide children between 12 and 18 in dormitory life and in their studies. Some of these children came to England with hopes and aspirations similar to those of my youth, while others were sent by their parents who hoped that life in England would benefit them. Daily in my work, I had many encounters with the young shoots from Japan and I loved them and suffered with them. The difficulties and the pain the children experienced were largely the illness of our society, which I knew well in my teens. I gave all the support and encouragement I could. However, my idealistic view of life and education was constantly challenged by the different reality of the children's background as well as by the norms and demands of Japanese society. Before I had any symptoms at all, after one year had passed, my doctor diagnosed an early stage of cancer in me. I was hospitalised, operated on, and sent to convalescence.

On the physical level, my first experience of illness passed without much pain or difficulty. Yet my soul knew its meaning: I was losing sight of my own wish.

From Park Attwood to the Centre for Social Development

In the snow-covered garden of Park Attwood, where my friend urged me to go, I learnt how to be. While practising my slow walk in the frozen world, I conversed with Carolyn, my Canadian friend who died of cancer shortly before my hospitalisation. Another friend had been fighting cancer in Japan. (I received the news of his death as I went back to work a few months later.)

My gaze often rested on a tree in the garden and soon I was in conversation with it as well. Finally I stared painting the tree which moved me with its message of living. I saw how it balanced its heavy boughs in perfect poise between heaven and earth. It was wonderful to witness its preparation for spring – its countless tiny branches slowly turning red at the delicate tips. When I noticed that all the tips of the branches were gently curled up towards heaven, their gesture of life shook my consciousness and I woke up from the spell. While painting it from my window, I promised myself to seek for the life-giving vision and to pursue my quest to the end.

Nearly five years have passed since that wintry scene. I picked up a copy of *The Inner Aspect of the Social Question* from the shelf of Park Attwood and it led me to anthroposophy. It gave me the inner strength and vision I needed to continue my search. An active elderly anthroposophist initiated me one summer into veil painting, which firmly connected me to the source of my creativity and I found a painter in me. After some hesitation, when I took my paintings to the school festival exhibition, my most difficult pupils responded to them and opened their hearts, as if they had been waiting for it. The warm response of the super modern youth of Japan touched my heart, with what felt like the gentle touch of angels.

Biographies

I found I was ready to live for my deepest self. I left my work and joined the Biographical Counselling Course at the Centre for Social Development in early 1997. From Epiphany to Easter, I rejoiced each day together with 16 others from all over the world. During the four years at the Japanese school (and long after that) in the numerous occasions spent with suffering souls, how often did I feel the need for deeper knowledge, for healing and for the gentle tool to handle fragile, almost broken hearts? With them, my own heart was seeking for the light, for the vision, for the way forward through the Ahrimanic forces of our times. Was it then surprising that in the first weeks of the course, the theme, which I was vaguely aware of, was brought to me by my former pupil C? On my visit to the school one weekend, she confronted me gently with a recent incident involving a young British history teacher. In his lesson, he said, "the use of the atom bomb was the right move, for it ended the War." C unsuccessfully tried to protest to him, for her grandmother was there in Hiroshima when the bomb was dropped so long ago. But in the heart of this young girl of 17, it was still a vivid memory of horror and the pain of fresh wounds. C was hurt deeply by the teacher's words, troubled by his views and was having sleepless nights. She was in fear, in despair. I wanted to support her from the depths of my being. I reminded her of her wish to study abroad, to learn the basic skills which would be helpful for the world community. I assured her that a gesture of healing and uniting would bring a better tomorrow to the world. In my memory of the recent past was another girl who shared with me her pain and fear of the atom bomb, which she was carrying in her young soul and body. Her wish was to work for the world community as well.

History

I also recalled several precious dialogues I had had a year before with Jewish and German people, for they also were carrying painful memories of the sufferings of their families during the last war. I realised that the War was not an event that had ended in the past, but was still here in the middle of our lives. These memories and pains were moving the generations who came after the war towards their destinies today. My thoughts naturally turned inward and I saw my father who had been in the last war as an officer. Now I was fully aware of the atrocities of the Japanese military.

In the following weeks when we looked at our biographies, those thoughts intensified. A small painting of my father's first spoke to me. "Who was he?" What was he thinking when he painted "The Gate of Heavenly Peace" in Peking between periods of duty? My father was a good painter and I grew up looking at this painting which my mother had put on the wall of our living room. A courageous young major and a sensitive artist. I found it hard to bring the two images of my father together. The memories of many more pictures of his, which I saw in my student days, came back and spoke to me. In my imagination I saw him drawing his injured friend while he was recovering from his own injuries. I saw him painting a serene lake in the countryside in spring in Toyotsu. It must have been the painting of his adolescence before he went to war.

My picture of that period of Japan – just before the world went to war – started changing when I placed this young boy with a brush in the glowing spring scene of his home village. "What were his dreams and hopes?" "How did he feel when he went to battle for the first time?" and "How did he see his life and the world in the chaotic period immediately after the war?" Question after question came to me and I saw him more vividly. Then his answer, which I thought I'd never be able to hear, came; it was in the selection of books he bought when life became settled several years after the war. It was also in the memory of my mother's – "Your father turned down the invitation to join the self defence army, saying the war is over and we are in the new age of peace". When I came to see the warm gaze with which he took countless photographs of his family, which he developed himself in the improvised dark room in our small flat, I felt connected to my father. I saw the connection. The past is shaping the present and the future. In order to create the future of light, we must own our past, learn from it, and be fully aware of its power over the present. I felt history was asking to be examined in the clear light of today so that its countless mistakes could be remembered, its numerous wounds be attended to and healed at last.

Revelation

"From where does healing come?" I felt this question had been with me for a long time. Easter was approaching and the end of our Biographical Counselling Course. During that week, the participants presented their research projects. I chose the biography of 20th century Japan. I wanted to show the movement of the Japanese Folk Soul working with the Time Spirit. However, when I looked into the lives of five individuals I realised right in the centre of these lives was the atom bombing of Hiroshima and Nagasaki. After the presentation, I stood by the lily-pond of the Centre for Social Development and asked myself, not for the first time, "Why was I, as a young child, not frightened by the sight of the death of my father?" "What was it that I felt in that hour...?" Then I knew. My father's love protected me and guided me. My heart was warm as I took in the answer. At that moment I saw the picture I feel could connect the broken pieces of humanity into the whole.

Christ intervened at the moments when atom bombs touched the Earth in the summer of 1945 in Hiroshima and Nagasaki. People suffered, died and are still in pain but where is the hatred, anger and revenge in the younger generation from Hiroshima and Nagasaki? It's not there. Instead, their dreams and wishes are for unity, for love.

All my understanding of the New Christ experience is met in this new picture of Hiroshima and Nagasaki. And Nagasaki was the first Christian land in Japan where many suffered long before 1945. In the XVII century, the rulers of Japan closed the country to the rest of the world, for its intuitive leaders of that era saw that Christianity was finding the way to the hearts of peasants in Nagasaki. The rulers suppressed Christianity, and people bore the suffering with courage, and many died carrying the cross in their hearts.

Japan, Japan

In the course of my life, I often wondered about my relation to Japan, the country of my birth, for my view of life was very different from those who were around me. I had been aware of the importance of "Ego" which was not welcome in the society and culture of Japan. Yet I felt it was my treasure, my torch in the journey of transitory earthly life. Through my ego, I felt, I was connected to the greater cosmic forces, the spiritual world. I needed more time to know the meaning of my connections to Japan where I had chosen to be born. I needed to walk many more lands, to meet many more souls, which I did. In the process, I came to realise the countless gifts Japan had bestowed on me. The Nature Spirit of Japan, for instance, nurtured and inspired and sustained me throughout the desperate times of my life. It enriched me and taught me how to be in tune with the Nature Spirit of other lands. Throughout my journeys, I never felt lost, for I felt the deep embrace of the Nature Spirit of each place, and I was at home.

The quality of its gentleness is reflected well in the Japanese people's nature. And I perceive the essence of Japanese people to be spiritual even when the country is seen as dominated by the present materialistic society. It is not easy to explain this; so by writing part of my life story I hoped to answer the question.

In relation to Japan, I'm experiencing a mystery of existence, or of life. Now that I live far away from Japan, I feel my connection to Japan and its people is deepening and I am very grateful that it is happening this way.

Courage to Heal

During the past months, I created my work of advisory services, which I named Sophia, for she was the Spirit which was guiding me. Every step was new and uncertain but it took me to the place I needed to be. In the process I learnt how to be true to my intuition. On the way, I witnessed unforgettable moments, which shine on my path. I end this story with one such moment I experienced this summer, for it is a story of healing of our time.

At the end of May in Emerson College, four of us were sitting in a room with a large window, which presented a beautiful summer scene with wild flowers, and blades of grass shining in the sun. A young German woman was sitting face to face with a mature woman from Israel. Two of us – an American and myself – were sitting nearby as "guardians". We were practising a deep-level dialogue as part of the 2nd year training in Biographical Counselling. After a few initial comments there followed a silence. Then the German spoke, "I cannot help thinking how you are feeling sitting here with me – from Germany." I was shaken by her words, yet this was the question I often held within me when I was with a German and a Jew, though I was never prepared to voice it. I know that no one is really able to talk about "that time" in Germany even today. In Israel, it's simply too painful to mention. The woman from Israel was experiencing deep feelings which were visible, but kept silent for a long time. When I thought maybe she'd let the question pass, for its enormity, she spoke; "I was taken back to the past all those years ago, by your words. Though I did not experience the war directly, all kinds of feelings are stirred It was before you were born." "I was not there, but my country did such horrific things to your people". The tears welled up the eyes of the German woman and flowed down her cheeks onto her sensitive hands. She had been suffering…since when? Maybe all her conscious life. Even before. The Jewish woman kept her steady gaze on the German, 14 years her junior. In fact she looked extremely young… waiting for the heavy sentence for the crime she was not part of; yet because of her connection to her country, she would not be free from it in her consciousness. A multitude of emotions were fighting within the Israeli. My heart was beating fast. In the end, one which was stronger than the other expressed itself without words. That of acceptance and forgiveness. The incredible depth of warmth was radiated from her to the solitary brave German soul who could not suppress the question everyone preferred not to see. More than that, she was asking for forgiveness for the crime of her country. And the sincere, courageous Israeli woman turned to her (and us) with love. We held each other; for each of us came from the countries that had fought and killed each other's people…for what end? It was a ritual of forgiveness of the dark past and of healing. I now have no doubt that healing begins when one individual soul who suffered long is received by another such soul.

When I am granted to share an experience of this kind, I cannot help feeling my biography is a story of searching souls of our time, of those who hear the call of the Time Spirit. We live in a time when his call is so clear that those who hear it cannot fail to be moved. Towards the place of healing, of love. It is a fearful task to choose to live our individuality fully, yet courage to heal grows only in the firm soil of each individuality. And the joy of it is the knowledge that I share the burden and darkness of our time with so many earnest souls all over the planet.

Come Alive !

Sibylle Eichstaedt

Have you ever been in a situation where life puts you at a crossroads, where one of the choices meant leaving all your familiar ties and structure and venturing off into the unknown? Where there seemed to be an almost unresolvable battle between responsibilities towards yourself and responsibilities towards those ties – the painful search for the "karmically right thing"? And you had no idea what would happen next, guided only by a dim sense that what had been could not continue?

Not long after completing my training in speech-formation, I was invited to teach and co-direct at a speech training centre. This was a great gift and a privilege, enabling me to work full-time and develop in my new profession. It was an ideal work situation for me, and I threw myself into it with great enthusiasm and commitment.

The work grew, and after two years I was asked to take on a share of the management. During the following months this extra responsibility together with a number of challenges in my personal life provided a fertile ground for disruptive forces to creep in and undermine my vitality. Gradually, as I became more alert to what it takes to run a school, my fire of enthusiasm was weakened by anxiety. Artistic levity and playfulness were dragged down by the weight of actual and imagined responsibilities. Love for the work was invaded by fear of failure, and authenticity – as acceptance of oneself whenever one is in one's development – was undermined by unrealistic expectations of myself, wrapped up in so many "shoulds" All of this gradually hollowed me out, until I seemed to have no resources left. I was soon completely depleted and burned out. Even though I was steadily losing weight, my body felt heavier than ever before.

This state worsened, and at last my doctor suggested taking a year off. This caused a strange mixture of relief and terror that threw me into turmoil. One voice in me was crying out "Yes, pleeeease!" Another immediately began to fight, clinging frantically to the safety of regular work-life with all its familiar, established relationships and structures, and the security of an income. And, above all, wasn't I turning into a karmic deserter, messing up my destiny, and letting down the school, my colleagues, and the students? I had only worked there for four years, hardly long enough to justify a sabbatical.

I wavered back and forth between these two voices, the one very gentle and straightforward, the other complex, hyperactive and sophisticated. Even though I had developed a secret love for the first one, how could I be sure I was allowed to listen to it ? How could I be sure it wasn't a Luciferic temptation? It was almost as if I wanted the gods of destiny to appear in person and authorise me to take such a bold and dodgy step. In the end, however, my state of weakness left me no choice. I came to trust that things could only get better if I left, and for sure worse if I didn't.

Almost from the moment I decided to take a year off it was as if my life began to operate on a different frequency. It was as if a great blockage had got unplugged and destiny could flow again freely. My decision seemed to attract a series of events and encounters that I could never have anticipated. It was as if my step was not only affirmed but celebrated and blessed by the spiritual world through helpful coincidences and support from unexpected sources.

I immediately sent news of my sabbatical to all my friends. Within a week I received a phone call from a colleague in America telling me she had just been asked to start a new eurythmy initiative and asking me to join her in this pioneering project. Without having to "think" I knew instantly that this was what I had to do.

Within a week of making this decision, a "chance" encounter resulted in an offer of accommodation for my first few days in Colorado. When I arrived there my hosts took me to a neighbourhood garage sale run by a Korean lady. In the ensuing conversation she offered me a room for the duration of my stay saying she had a strong feeling that I was meant to stay with them as their guest.

This was the amazing overture to what was going to be a very rich six months in the United States. It was a time of new, strong, personal and professional bonds, and a time of delving deeply into artistic creativity, both of which steadily rebuilt my strength and reconnected me with the love I have for my work.

My visa not allowing me to stay longer than six months, I returned to England with no further plans for my sabbatical. Little did I know that in England, too, a whole new "karmic network" and field of activity was waiting to unfold. Searching for a place to stay, I ended up at an anthroposophical training centre which had spare rooms during the Easter holiday. I quite naturally got involved with the care of the house, two weeks later I was asked to stay as the house manager's assistant, and eventually replaced her during her sabbatical. My time there felt like a blessing as well as a dream come true. Balancing the speech work with this practical and social activity had always been a wish of mine, and here it had entered my life when I had least expected it.

When I then returned to the speech school full of strength and vigour, all the old symptoms returned forcefully, even without the old anxieties and fears. After the initial shock, I began to wonder whether there had been more at work than simply a temporary crisis. Was I losing energy because I was not in harmony with my karma ? Was the voice of destiny trying to make itself heard through my forces going on strike ? I suddenly knew without a shadow of doubt that I was not in the right place. I did not know why. There were no conflicts or problems, nor did I have any other plans that were drawing me away. However, I knew I had to go away and make place for whatever wanted to happen. Fortunately my colleague was supportive and said, "If it is karmically right for you to leave, then it will also be karmically right for the school." In spite of the sad good-byes, I felt deeply relieved.

Within a week of this decision I was called by the director of a Teacher Training Program in California who had no idea that I had just decided to leave the school, inviting me to come and give an intensive speech course. Soon other things came my way and fell into place, and before long the whole of the following year was filling up with work, particularly in the United States. And the school? Student enrolment has doubled since I left! It has flourished and gone through its own renaissance, just as its former teacher has !

During these last four years my professional and personal lives have become enriched and deepened in ways I could never have imagined. My work has been blessed with a new flow of creative energy, insiration and insight. And I have been much stronger and healthier, despite my flying-carpet existence.

All this touches on questions of health, where one is called to work, and who one's destiny companions are. Exhaustion and burn-out are widespread. People's constitutions – especially in my generation – do not seem to be so robust. Spiritual development awakens us to responsibilities to ourselves, to the world, and to vast cosmic vistas of evolution.

This can be elevating as well as daunting. How can we find healthy ways of keeping alive, of looking after ourselves and our "instrument"? How can we find ways of committing to our ideals and work situations that do not undermine our own well-being? So that there is no split between responsibilities to oneself and to the world? On one of my travels I came across the following quotation:

> Do not ask yourself what the world needs.
> Ask yourself what makes you come alive,
> and then go and do that,
> because what the world needs
> is people who have come alive.

How can we live so that "striving" and "coming alive" are not mutually exclusive ?

In meeting blockages in life, there is always the question whether they are a call to overcome them or to change direction. Faithfulness and loyalty to the given work-situation are often stronger than the inclination to leave. Such loyalty can become an end in itself, and block karma. Can we learn to listen to the voice of karma before it speaks the drastic language of illness? Have we the courage to enter an inner stillness where we can begin to hear the truth of a situation, and if necessary step into the unknown?

Book Review

From Gondhishapur to Silicon Valley
by Paul Emberson

Etheric Dimension Press 1996
ISBN 2-904991-43-3

Terry Boardman

I began this book with feelings of keen anticipation, for it seemed to promise a forthright anthroposophical treatment of one of the most pressing problems of our time, namely, how to develop a spiritual understanding of, and way of working with, technology, and that it would do this within a historical context that would illuminate the connections between the – in anthroposophical circles – somewhat vaguely comprehended 7th century Academy of Gondhishapur and the modern phenomenon of computerisation. I have to say that I ended the book with very mixed feelings: sincere gratitude to Emberson for his courageous work in tackling one of the most dangerous areas of spiritual science (he is, after all, not merely an author, but also director of Anthrotech, the research institute based in Switzerland and Scotland that is seeking to develop new forms of technology that are inherently moral); gratitude also for his casting fresh light on, amongst other things, the enormously significant roles of Francis Bacon and Alan Turing and on key aspects of the development of computer technology. But I was also left with a feeling of considerable disappointment, because this book falls far short of a successful treatment of its supremely important theme. There are simply too many gaps in its argumentation and too many questions left begging, especially since it does not, like some other anthroposophical books which deal with contemporary themes, seek to restrict its readership to those conversant with Rudolf Steiner's work.

But before considering the book's failings, let us look first at its strengths. It is a martial work, uncompromising, straightforward; it calls a spade a spade. One feels very much Emberson's Michaelic spirit boldly seeking to take its place in what he calls "a battle for the future of Thought" itself between Michael and Sorat, whom he refers to as the Binary Beast, the inspirer of binary computer technology. Emberson makes clear that computers are no morally neutral technical tools, but weapons in the armoury of the Powers of Evil. "Our study will reveal that the genius behind artificial intelligence is not human, and that the computer is the instrument of a specific spiritual entity (Sorat, the Sun Demon, or Antichrist) which is using it to bring mankind into its power." (p6) While urging no Amish or Luddite attitudes to technology, he points to the need for ever greater discrimination in the use of computers and electromagnetically-based technology in general.

The book's cover itself is a challenge to modern materialists: a computer chip bearing the number of the Two-Horned Beast 666 sits at the centre of a spider's web across a landscape that could be Mars but is supposed to be the south-western United States, the stronghold of subterranean Ahrimanic magnetic forces; one thinks of the massive stark and skeletal contours of the Grand Canyon and Death Valley, the deserts, buttes and mesas of New Mexico, Arizona, southern California and Utah. The eight chapters of the book are organised musically in the form of an octave, and the qualities of the seven intervals of the octave can clearly be discerned by the attentive reader. In this, Emberson matches form to content in that he emphasises the importance of countering the materialist notion of the world as consisting of individual building blocks (subatomic particles) which physicists with their ever larger machines go on searching for. He answers this with the spiritual scientific picture of matter as the final condensed form of cosmic music, the rhythms and patterns of the Harmony of the Spheres – an idea towards which quantum mechanics now seems to be groping, if only abstractly. The individual physical element thus emerges out of the collective, not the other way round.

The essence of Emberson's argument up to chapter five is perhaps contained in the following extract from the most martial chapter four:

"We see how the working of the Beast descends from the spiritual into the material. In the seventh century he would have given mankind all earthly knowledge through inspiration and revelation. In Bacon's vision, knowledge was no longer to be received through revelation, but was to be elaborated by man's mind, like a mill grinding flour. Then, in our century, came Turing's machine. It is supposed to be a universal machine, that can process all knowledge in all possible ways. Under the guidance of the Two-Horned Beast everything becomes twofold. All threefoldness is lost, destroyed. He is indeed the Binary Beast…"

Drawing from Rudolf Steiner's spiritual research, Emberson makes clear that the essence of Antichrist is black magic, that is, to turn the greatest spirituality on its head – the pentagram is inverted. In the pentagram 3 is above 2. The black magic pentagram has 2 above 3. In the pentagram the 5-membered man's head is above; in the black magic pentagram it is below. The head is thus obsessed with matter; one's brains are in one's boots. Emberson says that Sorat sought to pervert the wisdom of Mani, the greatest human initiate, whose stream of spirituality aimed to transmute evil into good – the epitome of white magic. Mani was born in Babylon c.AD 216 and put to death in Gondhishapur c.AD 276. After his death Mani called a spiritual council that laid the plans for man's development in the 5th Post-Atlantean epoch (1413-3573). Man would be enabled to find his freedom through the development of materialism; traditional revelatory spiritual knowledge would be closed off, but a personal connection to the spirit, ways to spiritualise natural science in particular, would be brought forward by the Rosicrucian movement. Mani's council aimed at all this. Sorat sought to frustrate these aims by destroying Rosicrucianism and driving mankind deeper down into materialism than it needed to go for the sake of its development.

The Academy which emerged in Gondhishapur after AD 500 was a hothouse of all the streams of knowledge from East and West which found their way to Persia, and this accounts for its extraordinary fecundity which Sorat sought to use for his own ends. Emberson describes how Sorat failed in the seventh century to precipitate man prematurely into the modern Consciousness Soul epoch via the Academy of Gondhishapur (at its peak in 666) by deluging man with inspired revelations that would place fantastic technical achievements in the hands of a morally underdeveloped humanity. Sorat then inspired Harun al Rashid in Baghdad (c.800) to take up some of the gifts of Gondhishapur, and then induced the Vatican to bring about the Council of 869 which effectively reduced man by a new dogma from a Trichotomy to a Dichotomy: body, soul, and spirit became just body and soul. Closing off the individual path to God via the individual spirit (traditional mysticism – the Way of the Orient) led seeking souls in the West to find God in Nature and opened the way for the development of western natural science. This was the situation c.1600 and into it incarnated Francis Bacon bringing his impulses from the 9th century and from his experiences in the spiritual world after death, when he had opposed the Rosicrucian impulses of the individualities who had been Aristotle and Alexander.

Emberson's discussion of the complex personality and actions of Francis Bacon (chapter 2) is the strongest and most illuminating section of the book. He shows how Bacon gave western humanity three 'gifts': he "broke the thread connecting man's thinking to the wisdom of the past" by attacking Aristotle and all the old authorities. Each man must find truth for himself by observation and empirical experiment. In doing this, Bacon was justified and was actually serving Rosicrucian goals. Secondly, he "gave men a vision of an earthly paradise created by science and technology". This gift was ambiguous in that man does need to gain greater control of the circumstances of his earthly environment, but not at the expense of forgetting completely about the spiritual world. His third gift, however, was wholly pernicious, and here Sorat succeeded in inspiring Bacon, for Bacon not only "annihilated the spiritual word" (the Logos, the ancient idea of the creative Cosmic Word), he also claimed that all knowledge expressed in words could be reduced to a binary code, a series of a's and b's, revealing this fully in 1623 (the year of a great Rosicrucian gathering in Paris) in his book *De Augmentis Scientiarum.* Emberson writes: "On the one hand, (Bacon) is serving humanity by rejecting the spiritual power of words, in order that men may use them in freedom. Yet on the other hand, he is the instrument of the greatest opponent of Christ, the Sorat, the Anti-Word, who causes him to go too far." (p44) In one of the most fascinating parts of the book he shows how the House of Salomon, the hierarchical governmental structure in Bacon's utopian New Atlantis is structured exactly like a modern computer; it is a living human computer! "Bacon's paradise is governed by a living data-processing system of strictly utilitarian nature…It is thus no exaggeration to say that Bacon is the father of the computer…What he invented was the ideal computer…(he) annihilated the spiritual power of the word, and gave men the binary code, on which all computer programming languages are based." (p56-7)

After Bacon, Emberson discusses the British mathematician Alan Turing (b.23.6.1912) who developed the universal machine, a functional binary computer in response to Hitler's use of military ciphers to serve his goal of world domination. Chapter 4 contains valuable insights about the nature of the key mineral silica in computer technology. He shows how silica, which in itself is a pure selfless mineral related to light (hence its manifold uses in glass manufacture), a mineral that supports our ego consciousness and does not have an affinity with electricity, was selected by computer hardware manufacturers who grew artificial opaque grey silicon crystals, and 'doped' them (the industry's own term) with homeopathic quantities of specific impurities in order to produce, not true conductors of electricity, but semiconductors. Here we see that not only is computer software (binary-based languages) of demonic inspiration, but also the hardware itself. Silica was deliberately chosen and corrupted. A true conveyor and servant of light was turned into a conveyor of 'fallen' or false light - electricity.

In chapter 5, the 'darkest' section of the book, Emberson goes on to describe how, in both software and hardware development, human intelligence can no longer cope with the complexity needed for computer technology. The scale and speed are now beyond us; we are beginning to entrust further development of the technology to the machines themselves, that is, according to Emberson, to the demons which inhabit the machines and inspire their 'thinking'. A single vast computer brain is rapidly spreading over the planet:

"One of the most widespread delusions of our time is that binary computers were developed by human beings to serve mankind. This is not the case. Binary computers were developed by the Ahrimanic double in man, to serve the Sorat and his hosts. Man was but the instrument of the double's activity...Men are lulled to sleep by visions of knowledge and power." (p127)

The Internet and the World Wide Web have of course greatly added to this lullaby. Before allowing his readers something of a resurrection in chapters 6 and 7 when he deals with moral technology, in the rest of chapter 5 he paints an oppressive picture of the depths to which materialistic, binary-based, electromagnetic 'dark technology' will go in the 5th, 6th, and 7th epochs. Humanity will increasingly divide into two races based on consciousness and morality; the prospect for most of humanity, who will continue to cleave to 'dark technology' is indeed grim. Sorat will soon facilitate the physical incarnation of his servant Ahriman who will tempt mankind with technically-produced clairvoyance machines. In America and Japan there are already techno-meditation centres where people wear headsets which give them visual, audio and even tactile pseudo-spiritual fantasies. The ultimate destiny of today's burgeoning computer networks is the earth-computer of the 6th epoch when men will learn how to transform the earth's magnetic field into a single computer web; today's world-wide web of PCs downloading information from the Internet which is said to exist in cyberspace is but a first clumsy intimation of this.

Finally, in the 7th epoch, the American era, the Moon will reapproach the earth prior to reuniting with it. As it does so, the materialistic race of mankind will grow ever harder. In a scenario more bizarre than the most imaginative of science fiction stories, the materialistic race of mankind will be forced to coexist with a horde of mineral-plant-robot spider beings which will be the incarnations of the materialistic thought beings that have thronged the sublunary sphere since the time of Bacon.

These thought-beings, Bacon's 'idols', will be like a plague of locusts descending on the earth and most of humanity will be forced by their own actions and thoughts to live among them, just as we, in the short space of a hundred years have already got used to living among slightly less chilling mechanical spiders – motor vehicles and computers. The hardening process will finally lead to such a condensation of evil that the War of All against All will break out and bring the seven Post-Atlantean epochs to an end. This is a horrendous prospect, but then so is that portrayed in the Apocalypse of St John. The spiritual world believes mankind to be strong enough to accept such knowledge. "Today" said Rudolf Steiner, "we must no longer recoil from descriptions such as these."(p150)

From this sombre crucifixion scenario, Emberson moves in his sixth chapter to a more hopeful account of a technological resurrection. But it is just here, unfortunately, although there are many problems in the first five chapters which will be touched on later in this review, that the book really fails to satisfy. For all Emberson's descriptions of the moral technology of the future are nothing but the vaguest of generalities. He says that it will have something to do with the Tau, sympathetic resonance, personal moral forces and the laws of the moral world, resonance between macrocosmic and microcosmic (personal) vibrations, "beings living like seeds in human souls are elemental beings that are nothing other than the soul faculties related to processes in the nervous system." But this is hardly the exact science he speaks about in the very first paragraph of his introduction to the book.. One wonders whether he is reluctant to give away secrets, and certainly, many of the great inventors of modern times who have challenged technological orthodoxies (such as Nikola Tesla and Viktor Schauberger) have met with sudden ends. He mentions Günther Wachsmuth's theory of formative forces without elaborating it.. On p207 he says "The clearest possible thinking is the only sure guide on the perilous path that stretches ahead", but in the last three chapters in particular he often does not give examples of this clear thinking. For example he quotes Steiner extensively on how the new moral technology will be based on the cosmic forces of the Pisces-Virgo axis – "These specific etheric forces (Pisces-Virgo) active in the earth sphere will power machines, wherein they will be brought into resonance with a driving force originating in the human soul." (p192-3), but these less than clear indications of Rudolf Steiner's are in no way clarified or even amplified by Emberson; he simply states them and leaves them. One would have hoped that someone who has been busying himself with this specific area of technology and Steiner's thoughts about it would have come to some ideas of his own to help us to understand Steiner's enigmatic statements.

There is virtually no discussion of moral technology in the 5th PA (Post-Atlantean era), only some very vague notions about working with the forces of the plant realm. Moral technology in the 6th and 7th epochs will have to be based on a common wisdom on moral subjects to the point where moral truths become as obvious as 2+2=4; there will be a need to feel others' pain deeply. Collective religious beliefs will have to disappear and be replaced by complete freedom in the religious sphere. Materialism will become an antiquated superstition. The ideas underlying the threefold social order and Waldorf education must come about if humanity is to be able to work safely with electricity selflessly. The "good humanity will have learned to use the powers of the mind and of nature to protect themselves" from the attacks of the materialists in the 6th and 7th epochs. This is all heartening, but is not dealt with in any detail. On p220 he points to the dangers of the electromagnetic sea within which we live today. Surrounded by electrical waves, our bodies act as antennae. Again, he quotes Steiner, saying the effect of all this will be to make us more stupid. Computer operators affected by binary radiation, will take the binary intelligence into themselves and in effect, become computers, but again, no clear evidence is offered for any of this. Elsewhere, he criticises scientists for talking only of abstract 'energy' and 'forces' instead of beings, but throughout the book he does little else himself except merely use spiritual names - Michael, Ahriman, Sorat etc. which is hardly any more enlightening than abstract labels. On p189 "...instead of looking behind physical substance into the musical relationships that are the last echo of the Harmony of the Spheres, we (he means scientists) gaze fixedly down into the sub-physical world, which by its very nature is evil.", yet on p195 we read : "...the specific character of a Michael Age, with its impulse to penetrate fearlessly into the dragon-realm of the subnatural forces, bears a special relationship to technology." Scientists may not realise it is a dragon realm, but they do penetrate it fearlessly, even if unaware of its spirituality. If they did not, they would be unaware, and quantum physicists now are becoming aware, that there are no ultimate building blocks and that physical matter is actually condensed rhythms and patterns, in other words, thoughts. They are inexorably approaching the idea of the music of the spheres, the thoughts of cosmic beings.

In chapter 4 (p134) he implies without meaning to that Ahrimanic demons are the same forces as those of the constellation of the Twins, where the origin of cosmic duality (including electromagnetism and binaries) is to be found, and says: "These matters must be mentioned, although we cannot go further into them in this book" . This is simply not good enough, because the question of the Twins can be felt to be a secret key to much of this book. The Twins inspired the 2nd Post-Atlantean epoch, centred in Persia, which focused on the struggle between Ahura Mazda and Ahriman. The Persian culture produced

Zoroastrianism out of which later came Mani, whose thought was much affected by Zoroastrianism. Gondhishapur lay in this same cultural area. Moral technology and indeed the whole Post-Atlantean epoch is to reach a kind of climax in the 6th or Slavic epoch which will mirror the 2nd Persian epoch as our 5th epoch (the Anglo-Saxon -Germanic) mirrors the 3rd Egypto-Chaldean epoch. The Twins hold before mankind the challenge to transmute duality into threefoldness, to find balance between polarities, the Christ between Lucifer and Ahriman. For all these reasons at least, it behoves the author to probe deeper into the mystery of the Twins than merely quoting verbatim what Steiner has to say about them.

These unclarities apart, the fundamental weakness of the book is that it does not make its intended readership clear. If it is mainly for anthroposophical readers, it might expect a generous reception, because anthroposophers are accustomed to bold sweeping statements and tenuous lines of reasoning, and there are many things in the book, some of which I have indicated, that many anthroposophers will find do indeed throw light on the problem of technology. But if the book is also intended for a readership not very familiar with Steiner's work – and the introduction would seem to indicate this – then the style and reasoning are highly problematic and could expect a nonplussed or even hostile reaction, firstly, because Emberson does not adduce any spiritual scientific research other than Steiner's, and as I have said above, he often does not take Steiner's indications any further but simply quotes them. This is not helpful even for anthroposophers. He might well claim that he has nothing else to say about the historical Gondhishapur because he is not a historian, but since the Academy is so germane to his argument, it is not unreasonable to expect him to look further into what it was, rather than simply quote what he finds in Steiner's work about it. He could at least have referred readers to the very interesting Mercury Press translation (1993) of *The Academy of Gondhishapur – Aristotle on the Way to the Orient* by Heinz Herbert Schöffler (German original Verlag Freies Geistesleben, Stuttgart, 1979). From Schöffler's book they would have understood that the Academy, far from being a product of something simplistic called 'Arabism' was actually a highly complex multicultural phenomenon that was predominantly driven by Christian Nestorians trying to work with the thoughts of Aristotle and Plato! In other words, the Academy of Gondhishapur is intimately connected with anthroposophy and Rudolf Steiner, but because of Sorat's influence, it became a perverted form of anthroposophy, as it were. This would actually have buttressed Emberson's argument, if he had referred to it, because it supports the idea of evil being a misplaced good.

The second reason why especially non-anthroposophers would be dissatisfied is that Emberson's reasoning is so extremely tenuous. For example, his argument rests on the claim that there is a line that goes from Gondhishapur to Harun al Rashid to Bacon then Turing and on to Silicon Valley, and what binds these together is what could be called binary or dualistic thinking inspired by Sorat, the Sun Demon, or Anti-Christ. But having established Bacon's paternity of the binary code, Emberson does not adduce any evidence to show that Turing was directly influenced by Bacon's binary thinking, or indeed that anyone else was. Neither does he discuss why Charles Babbage in the 19th century chose to develop his mechanical computers on a decimal rather than a binary basis. Who then was inspiring Babbage? Emberson states (p102) that Silicon Valley is the new Academy of Gondhishapur of our time, but the Gondhishapur Academy's speciality was actually medicine. One could well imagine that some of the modern genetics research centres such as the Rosslyn Institute might have just as much to do with Gondhishapur as Silicon Valley, but then Emberson might well argue that they are all inspired by Sorat, and certainly, southern California is more of a cultural hothouse than Scotland. Finally, just as there is comparatively little about the historical Gondhishapur in the book, so is there little about the modern Academy, Silicon Valley. An astonishing omission is that Bill Gates, Microsoft, Intel, Netscape, and the evolution of the Internet figure nowhere in the book. While the Internet boom had hardly started in 1991 when the first, French edition of the book was published, it could certainly have been included in the present English version.

Emberson chooses to end his book with the last written words Rudolf Steiner communicated to the members of the Anthroposophical Society before he died, which were, appropriately, a warning about the need to balance the exploration of the dangerous world of Subnature and electricity with an equal penetration into the Science of the Spirit. Emberson draws attention to the fact that Rudolf Steiner underlined the last three words of that final communication: "It is just by receiving in Knowledge this spirituality to which the Ahrimanic powers have no access, that man is strengthened to confront Ahriman within the world." (*Anthroposophical Leading Thoughts*, Rudolf Steiner Press, 1973) Emberson's thoughts about technology are worth the world's hearing. Indeed, they are vital for an understanding of technology, which since the application of electricity has, as he points out, become a monster that threatens to overwhelm us. But if Emberson is to put these important thoughts of his before the non-anthroposophical world, he will need to present his ideas much more rigorously. This is a valuable book containing valuable insights; it is a pity their presentation does not do them justice.

Book Review

Leonardo Da Vinci
Origins of a Genius

By David Alan Brown

Yale University Press 1998 £35
ISBN 0-3000-07246-5

Andrew Wolpert

This beautifully produced and superbly illustrated book deals with Leonardo's early work. David Alan Brown, Curator of Italian Renaissance painting at the Washington National Gallery of Art, examines the technique and compositional approach in Leonardo's first paintings and concludes that there was a gradual evolution towards the artist's maturity. This has not always been the received view. Brown has identified Leonardo's hand in previously unattributed work, and describes the technical and stylistic innovations evident in his earliest works as unmistakable signs of his genius, even if there is also evidence that he was not a fully-formed prodigy from the start. Brown contends that his "early creative leaps combined with missteps" (page 2) do not detract from the beauty or fascination of his early paintings, and he eschews the inclination to read Leonardo's works backwards, contending that the early paintings are to be seen in the context they arose out of, and not just as predecessors of the great late works.

The books begins with an exploration of the rivalry between Pollaiuolo and Verrocchio, and the oeuvre and techniques of the latter, whom Leonardo was apprenticed to.

Then amongst other details, in a lambent analysis of the different approaches in the painted rendering of creased woven fabric, and the effective use of yellow ochre rather than gold, Brown contrasts Verrocchio's knowledge as a craftsman with Leonardo's observation of optical effects. Here and elsewhere in the picture he discerns compelling evidence for the proposition that the pupil was responsible for significant parts of the London National Gallery *Tobias and the Angel* hitherto attributed to his master. Brown asserts that the dog and the fish in the picture, as well as much of the figure of Tobias, reveal brush technique, style and acuteness of observation that confirm Leonardo's participation. He goes on to suggest that Verrocchio may well have availed himself of his pupil's talents also in his sculpture.

Brown undertakes a masterly reappraisal of the Uffizi *Annunciation*, and discerns the unmistakable hand of the genius in this (now undisputed) picture, despite the many unsatisfactory aspects that point to a certain immaturity. It is only in connection with one of these apparent "mistakes" that Brown overlooks what is a formative example of Leonardo's genius. The often commented on spatially illogical position of the Virgin's right hand in relation to the lectern admits of an explanation other than the usual one of Leonardo's imperfect grasp of perspective. Such an alternative explanation is connected with the traditional importance in pictures of the annunciation of showing that Mary was "troubled at the angel's saying" (Luke 1, 29). This iconography is observed in a conventional, albeit muted, way by the Virgin's left hand. However, it is the contention of this reviewer that the same "troubledness" is effectively and innovatively conveyed to the viewer as an experience by Leonardo's intentionally disturbing spatial inconsistency of her right hand. Here the artist makes an early attempt at engaging the less or more conscious soul reactions of the viewer, a characteristic of his style that matures with his later works.

In reappraising the Uffizi *Baptism* Brown attributes a greater share of the picture to Leonardo than the already traditionally acknowledged angel. He contends that the figure of Christ and parts of the background are by Leonardo, and that in such increasing encouragement of his apprentice, Verrocchio can be truly described as the first of Leonardo's many patrons. This leads to the sensitive perception and most touchingly human understanding of the changing relationship between a teacher and a pupil who outshines him. "It seems altogether fitting that whereas Leonardo's Tobias looks up to Verrocchio's portrayal of the boy's guardian angel, the figures Andrea [Verrocchio] painted in the *Baptism* gaze with wonderment at those contributed by his pupil." (Page 145)

A particular interest of this book to readers of *The Golden Blade*, specially in the context of the theme of this issue, may lie in the author's approach to the phenomena he engages with. Leonardo's love of nature and fascination with the details and forms of movement in flora, fauna, anatomy, musculature, physiognomy, and the effects of light and wind, are all well-known and repeatedly evidenced in even his earliest works. Brown is to be credited with the same all-encompassing loving observation and ability to describe what he has noticed luminously. His intelligent appraisal of a mass of details makes for enlightening reading. The conclusions he draws are cogent, and arise organically from the observations he describes. Particularly the way he characterises the artistic dynamic between Verrocchio and Leonardo leaves the reader uplifted by the example of human sensitivity informed by scholarship, and sheds light on a formative destiny partnership in the origin of a genius.

The sub-title of this book is unlikely to lead those

interested in spiritual science to expect occult revelations or esoteric explanations. But this book is more valuable than one which offers only ready-made spiritual interpretations. The highly competent, rigorous, and matter-of-fact approach gives consistently inviting access to wide-ranging research, and the reader is thus empowered by the work of the author, but also left free. The possibility of understanding the esoteric significance of Leonardo and his work is immeasurably enhanced by a book such as this. The patient devotion to the minutiae of the art as it manifests in the sense-perceptible – the pigment, the line, the traces of the artist's techniques – are all necessary to substantiate what may arise as an inspired flash of "seeing a meaning". Then such an insight can be borne out by an accurate reading of what the hand of a genius, inspired by the spirit, has inscribed into the substance of the earth.

Notes on the contributors

John Alexandra is Executive Vice President and Chief Financial Officer of New Century Bank in Phoenixville, Pennsylvania. He spent eleven years at J. P. Morgan, the Wall Street investment banking firm, where he was Vice President. Previously he was a teacher for seventeen years.

Manfred Klett is a founding member of the Dottenfelderhof farming community near Frankfurt, Germany. He is currently Head of the Department of Agriculture at the School of Spiritual Science, Dornach, Switzerland.

Ken Gibson is a writer and lecturer in History at The University of Derby.

Sibylle Eichstaedt works with creative speech both as a teacher and reciter.

Fumiko Chikami works as a counsellor and educational consultant.

*Terry Boardma*n is a historian and eurythmist who has lived and worked in Japan, and now teaches English in the West Midlands.

Simon Blaxland-de Lange is a teacher at Philpots Manor School, Sussex, where he is currently Chairman of College and management. He is also a translator, and is working on a biography of Owen Barfield.

William Forward teaches French and German, Parzival, and Economics at Michael Hall School, Sussex, where he is also currently Chair of the College of Teachers.

Andrew Wolpert teaches at Emerson College where his work includes language, literature, and Italian Renaissance Art.

The Golden Blade 48
1996

THE IMAGE OF BLOOD

The Mystery of Blood
James Dyson

The Bleeding Wound of King Amfortas
Karal Jan Tusenius

D.H. Lawrence's The Rainbow, The Lion, and the Blood of Sophia
Andrew Welburn

Mithras, The Bull, and the Transformation of the Blood
Christopher Clouder

Of Blood and Money
Christopher Houghton Budd

Money - The Christ Blood of The Threefold Social Order
Jack Foster

Chosen Destiny
Rudi Lissau

The Golden Blade 47
1995

THE QUEST FOR THE GRAIL

The Matter of Britain
Richard Seddon

The Polarity of Parzival and Gawain
Frank Teichmann

The Emergence of the Grail Legend
Hanah May Thomas

The Temple of the Grail
John Meeks

Eschenbach and Michelangelo
Andrew Wolpert

"Redemption for the Redeemer"
Alex Naylor

The Play of the Planets in Eschenbach's
William Forward

The Quest in New York City in 1994
Barbara Francis

The Golden Blade 46
1994

CHAOS, RHYTHM AND FLOW IN NATURE

The Universe as Organism
Lawrence Edwards

Chaos Theory and Projective Geometry
Nick Thomas

Our Heart: Sounding, Serving, Unifying
Philip Kilner

Learning to Enhance Sense-perception
Olive Whicher

Flow Design Research
John Wilkes

The Golden Blade 45
1993

CHANGE IN A CHANGING WORLD

Celebrating Columbus
Paul Law

Upheaval in Adolescence
William Forward

Centring the Teacher
Dorit Winter

Mystery Play is Now
Christopher Marcus

Regenerative Grammar
Andrew Wolpert

Losing Ground
Ria Freiermuth

Finding One's Place
Stephen Briault

The *Flowering of the Soul in Florence*
Charles Lawrie

The Golden Blade 44
1992

EUROPE AND THE WEST

The Spiritual Contribution of the West
Virginia Sease

Language and Nationhood
William Forward

Are we detached ?
Andrew Wolpert

An Interfering Interest
Peter Tradowsky

Breathing and Circulation
Jenny Josephson

First Aid at the Turn of the Century
Jenny Josephson

Prometheus Unbound
Andrew Welburn

The Golden Blade 43
1991

EUROPE

Central Europe between East and West
Rudolf Steiner

The Spiritual Tasks of Central Europe
Sergei. O. Prokofieff

The Heart and Lungs
Jenny Josephson

The Emergence of Europe
Coenraad van Houten

For the Conscience of Europe
Charles Lawrie

The Soul and Spirit of a People
Athys Floride

Present Tasks of Central Europe
Manfred Schmidt - Brabant

In Memoriam for Adam Bittleston

The Golden Blade 42
1990

FREEDOM AND DESTINY

Man, Offspring of the World of Stars
Rudolf Steiner

The Observation of the Stars
John Meeks & Michael Brinch

The Life between Death and Rebirth
Elizabeth Vreede

The Bridge of the Green Snake
A. Bockemül

Rainer Maria Rilke
Rudi Lissau

Deeds in the Life of William Mann
Roswitha Spence

William Mann - The Teacher
Ted Roberts

Addiction as an Impulse towards Renewal
J. van der Haar

The Destiny of the American Indian
Brian Gold

The Golden Blade 41
1989

THE EARTH AS A SEED

What is the Earth in reality
Rudolf Steiner

David Newbatt- An Artist in Midstream
Carola Kindle

Three Great Ideals in our Time
Rudolf Steiner

The Light of the World
Owen Barfield

Technology and the Earth
Nick Thomas

Puppets Help in a Mixed-up World
Gisela Bittleston

Man and Nature in Different Cultures
Andreas Suchantke

The Many Faces of Water
Mark Riegner

The Powers of Sorrow
Georg Kühlewind